IMAGES OF WA

STILWELL AND THE CHINDITS

THE ALLIED CAMPAIGN FOR NORTHERN BURMA, 1943-1944

RARE PHOTOGRAPHS FROM WARTIME ARCHIVES

Jon Diamond

Pen & Sword
MILITARY

First published in Great Britain in 2014 by
PEN & SWORD MILITARY
An imprint of
Pen & Sword Books Ltd
47 Church Street
Barnsley
South Yorkshire
S70 2AS

ISBN 978-1-78383-198-2

Typeset by Concept, Huddersfield, West Yorkshire HD4 5JL.
Printed and bound in England by CPI Group (UK) Ltd, Croydon CR0 4YY.

Pen & Sword Books Ltd incorporates the imprints of Pen & Sword Archaeology, Atlas, Aviation, Battleground, Discovery, Family History, History, Maritime, Military, Naval, Politics, Railways, Select, Social History, Transport, True Crime, and Claymore Press, Frontline Books, Leo Cooper, Praetorian Press, Remember When, Seaforth Publishing and Wharncliffe.

For a complete list of Pen & Sword titles please contact
PEN & SWORD BOOKS LIMITED
47 Church Street, Barnsley, South Yorkshire, S70 2AS, England
E-mail: enquiries@pen-and-sword.co.uk
Website: www.pen-and-sword.co.uk

Contents

About the Author

Jon Diamond is an American practicing physician in Pennsylvania. He graduated from Cornell University and was on the faculties of Harvard Medical School and the Pennsylvania State University College of Medicine, achieving the academic rank of Professor at the latter. A lifelong student of military history, Jon has contributed numerous articles to Sovereign Media's *WWII History*, *WWII Quarterly*, *Military Heritage*, and *Civil War Quarterly*. He was a civilian attendee at the National Security Seminar at the United States Army War College in Carlisle, Pennsylvania. He has authored two Osprey Publishing Command Series monographs on *Orde Wingate* and *Archibald Wavell*. A forthcoming Osprey Publishing Combat Series monograph, entitled *Chindit versus Japanese Infantryman 1943–44* will be released in the near future. He is currently working on a book about the New Guinea campaign 1942-1944 for Stackpole Books. As a physician, Jon takes care of many Second World War veterans, who are becoming a dwindling cadre due to the inexorable march of time. We listen to and read about their exploits lest we forget.

Introduction

The Japanese juggernaut in the Far East and Pacific began the rise to its zenith after the attack on Pearl Harbor on 7 December 1941. Soon other Allied bastions, such as Hong Kong, Singapore, the Philippines and many other possessions, fell to Nippon's swift offensives. After the inglorious Allied retreat through Burma in the spring of 1942, with the ensuing capture of that entire country by Imperial Japanese Army (IJA) forces, China was to become wholly isolated from resupply by both sea through Rangoon and overland across the Burma Road, located south of Myitkyina. Only a dangerous air route over the Himalaya Mountains ('The Hump') from Indian air depots to Kunming and Yunnan in China's south-west kept Chiang's forces combating the Japanese in their several-years-struggle. Without military assistance, China would be compelled to surrender and the IJA's extensive Asian mainland forces could then be diverted to other Pacific war zones, possibly halting the nascent plans of General MacArthur and Admiral Nimitz's dual-pronged assaults there.

Myitkyina, the traditional capital of Northern Burma, is located at the junction of the Mogaung and Irrawaddy valleys and lies at the southern tip of the Himalaya Mountains, which the American Air Transport Command's (ATC) C-46 and C-47 transports had to fly over from India to south-west China. The Himalayas, which serve as the main topographical division between the Indian subcontinent and the Tibetan plateau, are the causal factor behind the wide and severe climatological variations in this part of Asia, which contributed to the dangers of flying over such terrain in rough weather and, at times, in unreliable aircraft. Due to the ubiquitous threat of Japanese Army fighters stationed at the Myitkyina airfield complex, these transport aircraft had to fly far to the north, then swing south to Kunming and Yunnan. The Japanese Army fighters that were mostly stationed in Burma included the Ki-43 single-engined 1941 model *Oscar*, with two 12.7mm guns and a service ceiling of over 37,000ft as well as the Ki-45 twin-engined, two-seated 1942 model *Nick*, with three 12.7mm and one 20mm guns along with a service ceiling of over 33,000ft. Using the more northerly route to avoid these fighters, however, the ATC transports dramatically increased their fuel consumption while also reducing the cargo payload delivered by these planes to China. Furthermore, the air route itself was narrow and its saturation with transports was soon approaching to deliver the requisite tonnage to assist Chiang's struggle with the Japanese. In a nutshell, this air-supply nightmare would persist as long as Myitkyina remained in Japanese hands.

In order to keep China in the war as well as expand the width of the air-supply corridor from India to Yunnan province (The Hump), the eventuality of building a new road and pipeline from Ledo in India to ultimately join the old Burma Road south of Myitkyina was apparent to Allied High Command. The Combined Chiefs of Staff (CCS) ordered Lieutenant General Joseph W. Stilwell to train Chiang Kai-shek's Chinese 38th and 22nd divisions in Ramgarh, India and, along with the 5307th Composite Unit (Provisional), also known as GALAHAD or Merrill's Marauders, capture Myitkyina. This Chinese-American force fought the IJA's elite 18th Division and took control of the Hukawng and Mogaung valleys through which the Ledo Road coursed to enter the Irrawaddy valley within a few miles of the railway and airfield hub at Myitkyina.

Coincident with Stilwell's mission, Brigadier Orde C. Wingate's plan (*Operation Longcloth*) was approved by his mentor and General Officer Commanding (GOC), India, Field Marshal Archibald Wavell, to penetrate his 77th Brigade deep behind the Japanese lines in Northern Burma in February 1943 and disrupt their lines of communication (LOC). Although *Longcloth*'s outcomes remain controversial, the ability of properly-trained British soldiers to fight and survive in jungle combat nullified the prevailing dogma of the IJA infantryman's superiority there. With CCS support, Wingate planned an even larger second Burma invasion with six brigades (*Operation Thursday*) for March 1944 utilizing: glider-borne and C-47 transport air-landing of infantry; 'stronghold' defensive areas to foster Japanese LOC interdiction; and the First Allied Air Commando's aerial attack and resupply capabilities to revolutionize remote combat without any direct sea or land-based LOC.

Stilwell's overland advance and the Chindits' *Operation Thursday* during 1944 defeated the IJA in Northern Burma and enabled the capture of Myitkyina airfield in a *coup de main* on 17 May 1944. For a variety of reasons, including Stilwell's refusal to use the excellent British 36th Division in his assault, an additional seventy-eight days were needed for Stilwell's Chinese-American forces to take Myitkyina town while the debilitated Chindit brigades and surviving Merrill's Marauders were evacuated to India after too many months of combat, malnutrition and disease, which decimated their ranks and future capabilities as fighting units.

The ever-pragmatic United States Army Chief of Staff, General George C. Marshall, although supportive of his protégée, also realized the potential pitfalls of Stilwell's mission to conquer Northern Burma and capture Myitkyina: 'The mission … given General Stilwell in Asia was one of the most difficult of the war. He was out at the end of the thinnest supply line of all; the demands of the war in Europe and the Pacific campaign, which were clearly the most vital to final victory, exceeded our resources … General Stilwell could have only what was left and that was extremely thin … He faced an extremely difficult political problem and his purely military problem of opposing large numbers of enemy with few resources was unmatched in any theatre.' Also, as noted by the official American historians of the China-Burma-India (CBI) theatre, Romanus and Sunderland, 'One of the noteworthy aspects of the North Burma Campaign of 1943–44 is that the logistical preparations, the planning, and the fighting proceeded simultaneously.'

Japanese troops cheer *Banzai* atop Mount Limay after conquering Bataan in April 1942. Allied military disasters transpired regularly in Asia and the Pacific during 1942. (*Bataan Nat. Arch. 111-SC-334265*)

Japanese tanks and infantry advances on a wooden 'corduroy' road past an abandoned British staff car. Britain's motor transport was a hindrance during the retreat from Burma in 1942. (USAMHI)

Japanese troops advancing on the outskirts of Mandalay in April 1942. Prior to the assault, Japanese bombers had reduced Mandalay to a 'smoking crater' on 6 April. (USAMHI)

From the port of Rangoon, Japanese infantry inexorably marched northwards to Mandalay and eventually to outposts on the Chindwin River across from Assam. *(Nat. Arch. RG-208-AA-247-D-10)*

British commanders decided to fight the enemy outside Yenangyaung after destroying the valuable oil wells to avoid Japanese capture. However, the British 1st Burma Division was routed on 16 April. (*USAMHI*)

General Joseph Stilwell, in his signature campaign hat (*right*), discusses with The Reverend Breedham Case (in pith helmet, *left*) and Captain Paul Jones (*centre*, wearing peaked service hat) the distribution of loads among the party's native porters. The relatively new American commander of the CBI was suffering the indignation of having to lead his party of over 100 out of Burma to India by foot. (*USAMHI*)

A series of twenty-three curves of the Ledo Road along a Burmese mountain's spine. Its construction during combat was an engineering feat and connected Indian supply depots with the Burma Road. (*USAMHI*)

A C-46 flies over the Himalayas from India to China's south-western provinces' air terminals. This northerly, fuel-inefficient and dangerous route was used to avoid interdicting Japanese fighters based at Myitkyina. *(Nat. Arch. RG-208-AA-Q-41)*

Snow-capped Himalayan peaks from a transport's window. Such terrain in rough weather and, at times, in unreliable aircraft contributed to the dangers of flying the Hump Run. *(USAMHI)*

A pilot boards a Ki-43 *Oscar* at Myitkyina. Interdicting the ATC flight route to supply China also compelled the American pilots to maintain a more northerly route over the Himalayas. *(USAMHI)*

A wrecked C-46 lies in a Burmese field. Japanese fighter interdiction, severe weather, Northern Burma's mountains, and aircraft flaws produced many ground crashes often referred to as the Aluminium Trail. *(USAMHI)*

The Quebec Conference (QUADRANT), August 1943. Roosevelt, Churchill and the CCS ordered Stilwell to complete the Ledo Road with his Northern Burma offensive and approved Wingate's expanded second LRP mission. (*USAMHI*)

At Cairo's November 1943 Sextant Conference, Stilwell (*centre back row*) secured *GALAHAD* from Wingate's operational control for his Northern Combat Area Command after badgering Mountbatten (*far right*). (*USAMHI*)

Brigadier Lewis Pick, in command of the Ledo Road construction project since October 1943, meets with Stilwell to go over progress on the road in April 1944. (*USAMHI*)

A US Army engineer supervises native labourers using jackhammers to carve out a section for the Ledo Road, a colossal feat of civil engineering during combat. (*USAMHI*)

Due to the numerous tortuous turns of the Hukawng Valley's rivers, army engineers with Chinese assistance built hastily improvised bridges to get combat troops and supplies to the front. (*USAMHI*)

Two US Army engineers inspect a section of a bamboo water pipeline, which accompanied a metal gasoline one to bring these essentials to the frontline and eventually south-western China. (*USAMHI*)

Chinese troops unloading sections of metal pipes for the gasoline pipeline that ran along the Ledo Road to bring fuel for Chiang's armies and General Claire Chennault's Fourteenth Air Force. (*USAMHI*)

Chapter One

Stillwell, Wingate and the Collapse in Burma, 1942

Stilwell

Joseph Warren Stilwell, born on 19 March 1883, graduated from West Point 32nd in a class of 124 cadets. Commissioned as an Infantry second lieutenant in 1904, he served in the Philippines during the Moro insurrection. In December 1917 Stilwell, fluent in French, was sent to France as chief Intelligence officer for IV Corps in General Pershing's St Mihiel offensive. In August 1919 he became the Army's initial Intelligence Division's Chinese language officer and after promotion to major, he left for Peking. To escape the headquarters boredom, Stilwell joined a road-building project as an engineering advisor several hundred miles to the south of Peking. For several months Stilwell absorbed all aspects of Chinese culture and language, and developed a keen respect for the hard-driving work ethic of the Chinese peasant labourer.

Stilwell had two additional tours in China. In 1924 he commanded a battalion of the 15th Infantry regiment, stationed at Tientsin, where he initially met George C. Marshall. In 1926, when civil strife between Chinese communists, rival warlords and Chiang's nationalist forces was reaching a crescendo, Major Stilwell was sent into the countryside to gather first-hand information about the extent of the unrest. By 1929 he was on his way to becoming a recognized expert on China in the eyes of his United States Army peers and superiors.

In July 1929, newly promoted Lieutenant Colonel Stilwell was asked to teach infantry tactics at Fort Benning, serving as second-in-command under the direction of his superior and mentor, George C. Marshall, then the post's assistant commandant. Stilwell taught his younger officers the art of solving problems on the field during the heat of modern battle. Marshall wrote of him that he was qualified for any command in peace and war, which was monumental language for Marshall. Stilwell's tour at Fort Benning ended in May 1933 and, while there, he earned the moniker 'Vinegar Joe' for his acerbic commentary. In January 1935, Stilwell received an appointment as Military Attaché to China and was promoted to Colonel on 7 July 1935.

From June 1939 through to December 1941, Stilwell commanded a brigade, then a division and finally III Corps in California. Shortly after the Pearl Harbor attack, Stilwell was ordered to Washington expecting a command to invade North Africa. However, with the United States declaration of war on Japan, China and the United States moved from being only Lend-Lease partners to active co-belligerents against Japan, with Chiang receiving supplies again via the Burma Road after it was re-opened by Britain. US Army Chief of Staff Marshall and Secretary of War Stimson knew that any American theatre commander for China needed to be fluent in Chinese as well as the personification of strategic vision, tactical inventiveness and, above all, an excellent trainer of men, whether they be American soldiers or Chinese infantry from that country's peasantry. Both Marshall and Stimson sought out Stilwell, an 'old China hand', to be that commander. Stilwell was sent off to CBI to command primarily an air-and-supply theatre, with a principal client being General Claire Chennault and his 'Flying Tigers' (as part of the US Fourteenth Air Force), although he yearned to lead an American Expeditionary Force on the Asian mainland.

Wingate

Orde Charles Wingate was born on 26 February 1903 in India and raised by his parents among the highly pious, scripture-reciting Plymouth Brethren sect. Through-out his childhood, like his siblings, Wingate was insulated from other children his age and this may help to explain his irascible, often anti-social behaviour toward both peers and superiors. At public school he feared no one and was able to endure both ridicule and hazing. Wingate's strict adherence to the Plymouth Brethren's credo was at odds with the Anglican majority at school and, coupled with his exclu-sion from mainstream school, life placed him in the same predicament as the Jewish boys who attended there, so creating an affinity early on with the 'sons of David' and later on with Palestine's Zionist movement.

On 3 February 1921, Wingate passed his examination for the Royal Military Academy, Woolwich and entered that august institution for 'gunners and engineers'. In July 1923, Wingate passed-out fifty-ninth out of seventy relegating him to the Royal Garrison Artillery with the 18th Medium Battery on Salisbury Plain and was promoted to full lieutenant in 1925. Wingate enrolled at the University of London as an Arabic language student in 1926, to qualify as an interpreter for a Middle East posting. Later that year Wingate wrote *Strategy in Three Campaigns*, examining the Russo-Japanese War, the Schlieffen Plan and Allenby's Palestine victory, the latter of which he lauded the British First World War Field Marshal for his skilful tactics and fleetness of mobility to overcome an opponent's numerical advantage in the Middle Eastern theatre.

Wingate served as an acting major leading an infantry company (*Idara*) of 375 men in the Sudan Defense Force's (SDF) East Arab Corps (EAC) in Kassala Province for his entire tenure from 1928–33. The EAC was headquartered in Gedaref, with

Wingate's *Idara* stationed in Kassala near the Eritrean border. This isolated backwater allowed Wingate to exhibit command initiative and develop military principles about small groups of soldiers surviving in a desolate, inhospitable environment, which would have been almost impossible for his rank in the regular British Army. Training, fitness and field craft became his credos, which would enable his troops to remain afar from their garrison without LOC. Marching his company 500 miles into remote areas of eastern Sudan, Wingate experimented with ground-to-air control with RAF Squadron 47 (B), heralding this emerging tactic for future commands.

In early 1931 Wingate led a patrol against Ethiopian poachers and slave-traders (*shifta*) in the Dinder and Gallegu river border country of eastern Sudan. On 11 April Wingate departed Singa, on the Blue Nile, with the widely dispersed announcement to reach Roseires due south. He soon deviated east to the Dinder river region as to deceive any spies who might be monitoring his course. This mode of deception would be standard Wingate fare for the rest of his career. In pursuit of the poachers, Wingate was impressed by their ability to scatter and re-form under the threat of attack, thus cementing the tactics of *dispersal and rendezvous*, which would be later employed with the Chindits in Burma during *Operation Longcloth* in 1943. Since Wingate knew that the *Shifta* could elude his patrol in the Dinder's brush if alerted, he devised tactics that depended on deception, surprise and selection of the best areas for ambushes. Throughout his career, Wingate would stress all of these tactical points. Furthermore, missions such as these emboldened Wingate further that he could lead men and survive in an unforgiving environment.

In 1935 Wingate was promoted to captain in the 9th Field Brigade stationed in Wiltshire and started studying for the staff college. Later that year he was posted to Sheffield as the adjutant to a Territorial Army formation, the 71st (West Riding) Field Brigade, Royal Artillery, again giving him a good deal of responsibility for his rank. In September 1936 Wingate was posted as an intelligence officer (GSO 'I') with the 5th Division in Palestine. This was not a tranquil assignment since an Arab revolt had started five months earlier and the British 5th and 8th Divisions had been sent into Palestine to restore order. After a peaceful interlude, on 27 September 1937 the Arab revolt was rekindled and within weeks the Arab insurrection literally blazed anew as the Iraq Petroleum Company's pipeline to Haifa was set on fire by saboteurs with regularity. General Archibald Wavell, the GOC, Palestine, now with only two infantry brigades to enforce order, relied on his own unorthodoxy to overcome the numerical odds and began to use the Jewish Supernumerary Police (JSP) to fight the Arab terrorists. Coincident with this, Wingate also advocated the formation of small units of soldiers to be used offensively against the Arab insurgents. From these seminal thoughts emerged the Special Night Squads (SNS) composed of Jewish paramilitary volunteers reinforced by small numbers of British troops led by British officers and non-commissioned officers (NCOs). Wavell needed a new tactical and operative paradigm and Wingate presented it to him as the SNS force. A patron-protégée relationship was forged between Wavell and Wingate, the latter receiving the Distinguished Service Order (DSO) for his nocturnal ambushes throughout the summer of 1938, which dramatically reduced the number of times that the pipeline was breached. Despite winning a DSO, Wingate's tenure in Palestine was waning as he was showing signs of mental and physical exhaustion by October 1938.

On 3 September 1939, when Britain declared war on Germany, his previous patron General Wavell became C-in-C, Middle East. In July 1940, Wavell cabled London to request Wingate 'to fan into flame the embers of revolt that had smouldered in parts of the Abyssinian highlands ever since the Italian occupation'. On 18 September 1940, Wingate was ordered to Africa, eventually reaching Khartoum to develop a force of Ethiopian rebels as well as some Sudanese regular troops to administer shock therapy to the nascent efforts that had been previously implemented to defeat the Italians in Ethiopia's Gojjam Province.

In early January, Wingate formally crossed the Sudan-Ethiopian border, naming his unit *Gideon Force* after the Old Testament biblical warrior who surrounded and defeated a much more numerically superior foe. Wingate's command, which totalled about 2,000 Sudanese and Abyssinian regulars, 1,000 Abyssinian guerrillas and an assortment of British officers and NCOs, ultimately defeated the 36,000 Italians in the Gojjam, who possessed armoured cars, field guns, bombers and fighter-planes. Wingate injected his creative leadership on this irregular force and when his own deceptive propaganda caused the Italian troops to overestimate the size of *Gideon Force*, they withdrew towards the Gojjam's capital, Debra Markos. On 6 February 1941, Wingate established the Emperor Haile Selassie's HQ at Belaiya south-west of Lake Tana and then advanced further into the Gojjam until finally, on 5 May 1941, Selassie re-entered his capital in a captured Italian car with Wingate leading the parade on a white horse. With Selassie installed in Addis Ababa, *Gideon Force's* campaign was not yet over. Wingate was ordered to take a portion of his *corps d'élite* and harass the withdrawing Italian troops. On 20 May 1941, Wingate sent the local Italian commander a letter informing him of the surrender of his overall superior, the Duke of Aosta, at Amba Alagi the previous day and gave him twenty-four hours to surrender to British troops or be confronted by his guerrilla forces. The following day a column of 10,000 Italians and Italian colonial troops surrendered to Wingate's considerably smaller force by the use of bluff. Wingate also excelled in the art of military deception, repeatedly misinforming his opposing commanders as to his strength, compelling the enemy to make hasty, incorrect decisions.

In Ethiopia, Wingate clearly exhibited his conceptual framework in the Gojjam highlands for the upcoming Burmese long-range penetration (LRP) operations, by which an independent self-contained contingent could interfere with enemy LOC, and by use of guerrilla tactics could ultimately force a numerically superior enemy to withdraw. Wingate's expedition into the Gojjam with *Gideon Force* was another fore-runner to his first Chindit mission, *Operation Longcloth*, in Burma in 1943.

Wingate's force was disbanded and on 4 July 1941, he unsuccessfully attempted suicide in a Cairo hotel. In fact, Wingate was also delirious from the effects both of cerebral malaria and of an overdose of the drug he was taking to combat it (*Atabrine*). On 22 July, a psychiatric assessment was conducted on Wingate, which deemed that the suicide attempt was the consequence of 'a depressed state to which he was prone, aggravated by malarial fever', and that he was no longer suicidal and had fully recovered his mental faculties. Wingate returned to England in mid-November 1941 and was also passed fit for active service by a medical board on 30 December 1941. At this time, Britain was about to suffer catastrophe after catastrophe in her Far East bases. Yet, despite all of this, on 7 February 1942, Wingate was to be relegated to a military backwater and received orders to proceed to Wimborne, England to take command of a battery in 114th Regiment, RA.

Collapse in Burma 1942

By the end of April 1942 it was obvious that Lt Gen Sir Harold Alexander's Burma Army could no longer hold a defensive line against the Japanese, who were advancing northward from Rangoon to Mandalay. Three Chinese armies (each equivalent to a British division) had moved into Burma from the Chinese province of Yunnan between February and April to help stem the Japanese surging tide. Chiang Kai-shek had put Stilwell in command of this Chinese Expeditionary Force. However, his Chinese officers were often insubordinate and Stilwell's commands were frequently negated by Chiang's own meddling with his generals in Burma. To complicate matters further, the Chinese forces were nominally under Alexander's overall command. Stilwell had arrived in Burma in March thinking to use his Chinese troops in a counter-offensive. With the general collapse of the entire Allied position in late April, Stilwell became worried about his staff headquarters at both Shwebo and Lashio, the latter being abandoned on 25 April with its personnel getting to China via the Burma Road before its capture by the Japanese. After sending out fifteen members of his staff at Shwebo to Calcutta by plane, Stilwell started his trek northwards to Myitkyina by motor transport. Discovering that the railroad to Myitkyina was blocked, Stilwell ordered the abandonment of all of his motor transport on 5 May and, after reaching the town of Indaw that same day, he turned his party of 114 American, British, and Chinese soldiers, Burmese nurses and a few civilians westwards to start the 'Walkout' toward the Chindwin River. Stilwell was not only racing the advancing Japanese but also the soon-to-arrive monsoon rains. By 13 May, Stilwell crossed the Chindwin near Homalin, which marked the last major water barrier to the party's escape from the Japanese and Burma. Less than thirty-six hours after Stilwell left Homalin, a large detachment of Japanese cavalry entered the town. Not one member of Stilwell's party was lost during the great trek from Indaw to Assam.

When Wavell became C-in-C, India, after the disintegration of the American-British-Dutch-Australian (ABDA) command in Java in February 1942, he was disturbed by the lack of morale among his forces in the Far East. The Japanese advance in south-east Burma had been swift and it appeared that the British-Indian defence line along the Sittang River was collapsing. Rangoon was in jeopardy and its evacuation imminent. At this point, Wavell summoned Wingate to Burma to join his staff. Wavell believed that Wingate's methods might help stem the unstoppable Japanese advance in Burma. Wingate arrived in Delhi on 19 March 1942 and as a colonel was sent to Maymyo to take command of guerrilla operations in Burma. There Wingate met Major Michael Calvert, RE, at the Bush Warfare School and was impressed by his fighting zeal and willingness to lead guerrillas against the Japanese. However, the deteriorating situation impeded Wingate's ability to direct the guerrilla units that were formed under Calvert in Burma since the Japanese had advanced to the Chindwin on India's eastern frontier. Thus, Wingate returned to Delhi at the end of April 1942 and wrote a memorandum to Wavell on 'Long Range Penetration' (LRP), which was to serve as his blueprint for *Operation Longcloth* in February 1943.

Clearly, both Stilwell and Wingate had very different career paths, although fundamental similarities with language proficiency, service as intelligence officers in foreign postings, and troop-training excellence, especially in small-unit infantry tactics, presaged the roles that these two officers were to have in Northern Burma in 1943–44. For Stilwell, his expertise as an infantry trainer would enable him to build a fighting corps from the 38th and 22nd Chinese Divisions that he would train at Ramgarh, India to fight General Shinichi Tanaka's 18th IJA Division. For Wingate, his 'behind the lines' stealth assaults in Palestine and leadership of Ethiopian guerrillas against the Italians coupled with acquired expertise in the concept and implementation of small raiding parties using air-to-ground supply methods, as well as his quasi-military tactic of deception would enable him to establish his doctrine of LRP against the 18th IJA Division in the jungles and hills of Northern Burma.

The Japanese 15th Army in Burma was typified by the 18th IJA Division, first under Lieutenant-General Renya Mutaguchi and then commanded by Lieutenant-General Shinichi Tanaka. The IJA prepared for war in tropical training environments. During the 1930s, the IJA ran a jungle warfare school on the island of Formosa. Practical modes for jungle combat were perfected including issuing headbands to soldiers to keep the sweat from pouring into their eyes while aiming their rifles; utilizing lighter weapons and loads for the hot, steamy climate; incorporating the terrain as an added dimension, such as getting off the trail or jungle track and using the verdant foliage to conceal flanking movements around the enemy. Stilwell, and more convincingly

Wingate, tried to imbue these Japanese jungle lessons on their troops who would confront the IJA 18th Division.

The 18th IJA Division's three regiments were garrisoned throughout Northern Burma and, thus, fought the Chindits during both the 1943 and 1944 campaigns as well as having contested Stilwell's Sino-American advance down the Hukawng and Mogaung valleys towards Myitkyina, which began in the late autumn of 1943. The 18th Division, during *Operation Longcloth*, was one of the best divisions in the IJA and garrisoned the area through which Wingate's columns moved. The men of this division were from the Nagasaki and Fukuoka areas of Kyushu, which is one of the home Japanese islands noted for producing a robust and bellicose warrior. The division's troops possessed élan, having seen heavy fighting in China. By 1941, the 18th IJA Division had accumulated as much operational experience as most Anglo-American divisions would acquire in the entire 1939–45 war. This division had taken part in the Shanghai-Nanking campaign of 1937, with Mutaguchi as a regimental commander, and other campaigns in China. When not demonstrating extreme condescension towards his seemingly inept Chinese opponents, Mutaguchi ridiculed his other vanquished enemy, the British, who he swiftly defeated in Malaya with his IJA 18th Division, culminating in the capture of Singapore. The vigour of the 18th IJA Division had been shown in the jungle blitzkrieg, which had won Malaya for the Japanese.

Lt Col Stilwell (*left*) and Col Marshall at Fort Benning's Infantry School in 1932 where Stilwell earned the moniker 'Vinegar Joe' for his acerbic personality along with Marshall's accolades. (*USAMHI*)

Col Stilwell (*far right*) as Foreign Military Attaché in Peking along with representatives (*l-to-r*) from Italy, Great Britain and Japan in 1935. Stilwell was considered the US Army's China expert. (*USAMHI*)

Army Chief of Staff George C. Marshall (*left*) and the Secretary of War Henry Stimson. Both arranged for Stilwell's mission to China and ultimately the battlefield in Northern Burma. (*USAMHI*)

General Claire Chennault originally led Chinese-sponsored American volunteers (Flying Tigers), which were engaging the Japanese with P-40s. After Pearl Harbor, Chennault commanded the Fourteenth Air Force, utilizing fighters and bombers. *(USAMHI)*

Stilwell and Field Marshal Wavell meeting in New Delhi. After the Allied ejection from Burma, Wavell was dubious, if not obstructive, about feeding and arming Stilwell's Chinese troops. *(USAMHI)*

American pilots man their P-40 fighters with noses painted as tiger sharks. Newer aerial tactics devised by Chennault and the pilots enabled these older fighters to successfully engage the Japanese. *(USAMHI)*

Reverend Case, a Burmese missionary (*l-to-r*), a local village chief, *Time/Life* photographer Jack Belden and Stilwell negotiate for guides and porters during the Walkout. (*USAMHI*)

A Chinese soldier and Burmese nurse with Stilwell's aide, Lt Col Frank Dorn, all work together regardless of rank to complete the raft's shelter to cross the Uyu River. (*USAMHI*)

Stilwell the pacesetter during the Walkout from Burma in May 1942. Despite being older and jaundiced, he ensured that his entire party would reach India without any deaths. (*USAMHI*)

Brigadier Orde Wingate poses in his ever-eccentric uniform and solar topee after his return to India in May 1943 after the completion of the controversial *Operation Longcloth*. (*USAMHI*)

Wingate in mufti stands with SNS troops wearing their pre-war denim fatigues with serge field service caps in Palestine, 1938. (*Author's collection*)

One of Wingate's SNS patrols returns to base after a nocturnal foray in the Galilee region combating Arab insurgents. Note the variety of uniforms and headgear. (*Author's collection*)

Col Wingate heads Selassie's procession into Addis Ababa, May 1941. Following are his unofficial brigade major, Avraham Akavia, then Patriot Army members and finally the emperor in a captured motorcar. (*Author's collection*)

At Maymyo's Bush Warfare School, Wingate met Major Michael Calvert (seated, *second from right*), a sapper, who was to become Wingate's future column and then brigade leader during both Burma invasions. (*USAMHI*)

Slim's Indian troops, retreating from the Japanese, await an imminent attack in their trench on the Sittang River. These positions cracked and the Burma Army continued its retreat. (*USAMHI*)

Clearly demonstrating the élan, a Japanese infantry detachment marches across a typical Burmese steel girder, wood-planked bridge in Central Burma in spring 1942. *(USAMHI)*

Under the cover of smoke and artillery fire, a Japanese infantry unit advances rapidly in a Burmese town behind its sword-wielding officer. *(USAMHI)*

Japanese rapid-firing field pieces in support of infantry assault in Burma in 1942. The unit is a reinforced artillery platoon. (*Nat. Arch. 111-SC-144002*)

Japanese field artillery was antiquated since it was the infantry's tactic to rapidly advance against the enemy, thereby outrunning one's own artillery support.
(Nat. Arch. 111-SC-135340)

Japanese crew fires heavy (used 7.7mm cartridge) Type 92 machine-gun in Burmese hills. As a direct-fire gun for infantry, it had a range well over a mile.
(Nat. Arch. 111-SC-136339)

(*Above*) Indian Mountain Artillery Battery in action near Maymyo 1942. These artillery positions were routed by the advancing Japanese offensive after becoming isolated from their infantry. (*USAMHI*)

(*Opposite page*) Japanese heavy weapons detachment emerges from Burmese jungle. A paralyzing tactic against the Allies was to take a jungle path to get ahead of road-bound motor columns and set up road blocks. (*USAMHI*)

Chapter Two

Burmese Terrain

Any operation in Burma had to logistically confront the harsh reality of the climate and terrain. Regarding the weather, Burma is typical of countries in South and South-East Asia in that its rainfall is dictated by the Indian Ocean's monsoon winds. The monsoon lasts from mid-March to mid-October and as much as 220 inches of rainfall can occur when the winds change to the north-east. Rainfall is at its heaviest throughout Burma from June to August. Mud would become ubiquitous and roads and rudimentary dirt airfields flooded.

Burma is surrounded on three sides by mountain ranges covered in thick jungle and possesses the most varied terrain of any nation in South Asia. The varying altitude, which serves to create the country's climatic zones, includes jungle, hills and plains. Numerous upland areas are 3,000ft above sea level, while the Chin and Naga Hills to the west towards the Arakan and India are 8,000 and 12,000ft high respectively. There are also mountain ranges to the north and north-east towards China rising to over 10,000ft. The valleys in central Burma open out into thickly wooded plains dotted with low hills. Around Mandalay is the country's central plateau with arid and sun-bleached tableland. To the north of Mandalay, where Stilwell and the Chindits would campaign in 1943–44, the steep snow-capped spines of several mountain ranges, which include the Himalayan foothills, start their ascent from the Burmese forested lowlands. Often routes over these mountains were not wider than a column in single file and because it was nearly impossible to have supplies air-dropped, the Allies required mules and horses to carry the heavy equipment and supplies. Obstacles to the troops on both sides included the wild vegetation – 12-ft tall razor-sharp elephant grass, dense bamboo forests and mangrove swamps – wild animals – such as elephants, tigers, leopards, panthers, rhinoceros and crocodiles – and venomous snakes, and produced non-battle casualties. Likewise, disease-laden mosquitoes, poisonous scorpions, biting flies and leeches infested the impenetrable forests and swamps.

Burma at a glance of a map is an elongated central plain through which the main river systems of the Irrawaddy and Chindwin flow from north to south. Burma is traversed by four formidable rivers that run mostly in a north-south direction into the Bay of Bengal. The Chindwin River, where Wingate's Chindits initially marched and crossed into Burma during *Operation Longcloth*, has a breadth of 400 yards of fast-flowing water and forms the border with India. The Chindwin rises in the Himalayas to the north and is also a major southern tributary of the Irrawaddy River to the south of Mandalay. The mighty Irrawaddy River is 1,300 miles long and up to 3 miles wide in parts and it links Northern Burma with the sea. Its major northern tributary is the Shweli River, which joins it at Inywa. The Irrawaddy, lying at the very heart of Burma, is navigable by steamer from the southern delta for 900 miles to Bhamo. North of Bhamo the river continues past Myitkyina and Fort Hertz, navigable by only country boats and rafts. The horseshoe of mountains does, however, protect the Irrawaddy delta, which gets only 60–100 inches of rain per year, from the damaging floods experienced in parts of South-East Asia.

Particularly germane, on the Irrawaddy's eastern shore, the landscape changes and, instead of jungle mountains with a canopy and ample hiding or ambush spots, the terrain becomes a hot, extremely arid, water-less hardwood forest during the Burmese dry season. Wingate learned this upon crossing the Irrawaddy in 1943, with the terrain being intersected by roads the Japanese could patrol by vehicle. For the Chindits in *Operation Longcloth*, Wingate realized that the terrain was working against him and he had pushed into Burma too far. The Japanese, sensing that the Chindits might be trapped in the Shweli bend, continued to step up patrols east of the Irrawaddy with, soon, two full Japanese divisions searching for their columns.

Further to the east flows the Sittang and Salween rivers. The Sittang runs along the border with Thailand and runs east of the jungle hills of the Pegu Yomas. This river is nearly impossible to cross because of its strong tidal current. The Salween River rises in China and essentially forms the border with that country as well as the Thai frontier. The Salween River is longer than the Irrawaddy but is not navigable.

276388

(*Above*) Jungle-clad mountain ranges surround Burma's river valleys causing a varied terrain. Uplands are 3,000ft above sea level, while the Chin and Naga Hills are 8,000 and 12,000ft respectively. (*USAMHI*)

(*Opposite above*) For Allied troops operating near villages isolated in the Northern Burmese highlands, only air supply was often feasible to replenish rations and ammunition. (*USAMHI*)

(*Opposite below*) Undulating Burmese hills ascend over the wide river valley below. A bridge, appearing as a slender strand, traverses this river. Burma possesses four formidable rivers that run mostly in a north-south direction into the Bay of Bengal. (*USAMHI*)

Northern Burma also possesses sparse plains amid heavily forested low hills as shown by this Chindit waiting near a parachute marker to signal a low-flying transport to drop supplies. *(Nat. Arch. BIZZ 918 LA)*

Northern Burma's Himalayan foothills with their spines dwarf this multi-purpose L5 aircraft. In 1943, Wingate espoused that Burma's jungle canopy and mountains would obscure Chindit movements to disrupt IJA communications. *(USAMHI)*

The Chindwin's fast-flowing water forms a border with India. Retreating to Assam in May 1942, Stilwell (*right*, with stick) watches his party's dugout cross the 400-yard wide river near Homalin. *(USAMHI)*

Stilwell's Chinese troops ferry supplies across the Tarung River, a tributary of the Chindwin, on a narrow wooden raft in the Hukawng Valley to combat the entrenched IJA 18th Division. (*USAMHI*)

To cross the 3-mile-wide Irrawaddy in 1944 at Tigyaing (as Column 5 did during *Longcloth*), 36th Division soldiers lashed four motorized dugouts together and placed a raft across the midsections. (*Nat. Arch. 111-SC-201144*)

Lake Indawgi, a large lake in Northern Burma, accommodates an RAF Sunderland Flying Boat to evacuate wounded and sick Chindits of 111th Brigade from the *Blackpool* stronghold. (*USAMHI*)

(*Above*) Chinese artillerymen drag their 75mm pack Howitzer through the tall elephant grass to a new position in the Hukawng Valley. (*USAMHI*)

(*Opposite above*) Razor sharp tall elephant grass could tear at a soldier's clothing and flesh as well as provide concealment as this Chindit column marches through it in single file. (*USAMHI*)

(*Opposite below*) The more diminutive Japanese soldiers concealed by the elephant grass while their officer mounted on his horse is above the vegetation. A Burmese pagoda in the background. (*USAMHI*)

(*Above*) With the onset of the monsoon season from May to October, transport was a nightmare. Chinese troops plod through shin-deep mud once the Kamaing Road. (*Nat Arch 111-SC-274535*)

(*Opposite above*) A bulldozer pulls a truck and trailing 105mm Howitzer from a Mogaung Valley flooded field during the spring's monsoon season as these troops advance on Kamaing in 1944. (*USAMHI*)

(*Opposite below*) General Tanaka wanted mud to slow the Allied advance in 1944. A 2½-ton truck's front wheels are submerged into the Kamaing Road's mud during the late spring's rains. (*USAMHI*)

Lying on stretchers in ox-pulled carts, Allied wounded are brought 5 miles through rain-soaked tracks to the Myitkyina airfield for evacuation. *(Nat. Arch. RG-208-AA-12J-2)*

In order to help pull supply- and equipment-laden carts along jungle tracks, bullocks were used. One is loaded easily onto a C-47 transport here. *(Nat. Arch. RG-208-AA-11L-2)*

During the rainy season transport through water was a problem. Stilwell, in the first Jeep, crosses a swollen stream in the Hukawng Valley. *(USAMHI)*

To get supplies and heavier infantry weapons across rivers and streams, mule teams had to be coaxed to cross the waterways, as this Chinese column is about to do. *(USAMHI)*

The Burmese hills often had only narrow, rocky tracts requiring lengthy mule trains to march uphill in single-file with heavy loads on the animals. (*USAMHI*)

Chindit columns during *Longcloth* and *Thursday* avoided motor transport for secrecy and mobility, thereby relying heavily on animals to transport supplies and equipment as this Gurkha mule train shows. (*USAMHI*)

American ground crew load a reluctant mule onto C-47 transport for flight into Burma. Wingate severed the animal's vocal cords to prevent braying in the jungle. *(USAMHI)*

Chinese and American ground crews ease horses up planking onto C-47 transports lined-up wingtip to wingtip for flight into Burma. *(USAMHI)*

A Chinese muleteer with three of his charges on board a C-47 transport for the flight into a Burmese landing field. *(Nat. Arch. 111-SC-205040-S)*

Chinese 22nd Division troops attack Japanese positions in the dense jungle vegetation of the Hukawng Valley, with many bamboo trees toppled. *(Nat. Arch. 111-SC-266085)*

Americans inspect the structure of a Japanese bunker which used terrain features for camouflage and strong logs at the base and on top to resist both small arms and light artillery fire. (*Nat. Arch. 111-SC-166771*)

With stream depth rising and falling, improvised bamboo suspension bridges had to be hastily erected in the Naga Hills for Chinese troops to cross into the Hukawng Valley. (*Nat. Arch. CAM 700800 WP*)

Japanese infantry skirmish with Chindits during *Longcloth* in dense jungle. Wingate utilized the jungle overgrowth to conceal his Chindits from the more numerous Japanese and offer quick safety with dispersal. (*USAMHI*)

Well-camouflaged and pack-laden Japanese troops on muddy Burmese riverbank. It required tremendous strength and endurance to extricate oneself from the mud to get to awaiting ferries. *(USAMHI)*

Chapter Three

Stilwell's Chinese Troop-Training at Ramgarh and Allied Weaponry for Burma

The initial command structure in the China-Burma-India (CBI) theatre produced a sharp contrast and clash of wills between two of the principal Allied leaders, British Field Marshal Archibald Wavell and his American counterpart Lieutenant General Joseph W. Stilwell, which led to a political/diplomatic rift in New Delhi. Wavell did not share Stilwell's strategic optimism for a counter-offensive in Burma so soon after the inglorious evacuation of 1942. At an Indian press conference after his escape from Burma in April 1942, Stilwell plainly stated, 'I claim we got a hell of a beating. We got run out of Burma and it is humiliating as hell. I think we ought to find out what caused it, go back and retake it.' Wavell respected Stilwell, however, did not realize the manic goals and desires that the American was trying to achieve, namely reforming his two good Chinese divisions, which had escaped to India (the 38th and 22nd), as well as creating another thirty Chinese divisions from troops sent to India by Chiang's corrupt and incompetent military hierarchy.

As well as having vastly different backgrounds, Wavell and Stilwell harboured very disparate views on the use of Chinese troops in Burma. On 12 December 1941, Churchill informed Wavell that with the outbreak of war with Japan, he was now responsible for Burma. At Chungking in early 1942, Chiang Kai-shek offered Wavell two Chinese armies for use in Burma (a Chinese army was equivalent in size to a British or Indian Army division). Chiang's offer was not out of altruism, but his willingness to commit large Chinese forces was to maintain the Rangoon-to-Burma Road LOC, his lifeline. Wavell accepted only one army and he asked that the other, which was assembling around Kunming, stay there where it would be best-placed to move down into Burma if needed. Wavell also declined the second army because he, along with the War Office and Far East Command, had assumed that it was unlikely Burma would be attacked before the Japanese had consolidated themselves in Malaya and the Philippines. Also, there seemed to be enough Commonwealth and British troops in transit to defend Burma. Wavell further reasoned that since the Chinese armies had no administrative services, they would overwhelm transport and food supplies once in Burma. Nonetheless, at Chungking, his decision had the appearance of spurning the offer of Chinese help and inflicting a loss of face on the *Generalissimo*. It had seemed correct to Wavell that British and Commonwealth troops should first and foremost defend a country of the British Empire. Although not stated, Wavell lacked confidence in the Chinese troops offered to him, especially with their divided loyalty to Chiang. Wavell's main argument was that Chiang insisted on his troops being held together and not mixed with the British like Australians or New Zealanders, as the former Middle East C-in-C was accustomed to.

The only place where Stilwell was able to train Chinese troops for an invasion of Burma was at Ramgarh, India. This occurred over the protestations of many ranking British soldiers, especially Wavell, again mainly for logistical and quartermaster reasons. Ramgarh was officially opened in August 1942 with the 9,000 survivors of the Burma campaign that had walked out after the defeat. A large proportion was in the hospital, ragged and half-starved as well as disease-ridden with malaria, amoebic dysentery and potentially fatal Naga sores, the latter caused by the heads of leeches being left under the skin upon removal. Getting appropriate medical treatment, vaccinations and adequate nutrition, the average Chinese soldier gained over 20lb in the initial month at Ramgarh. Also, these soldiers received uniforms, helmets, weapons, and eventually training in artillery, Bren carriers and American M3 light tanks.

As Ramgarh received additional Chinese recruits from Chiang, on average 40 per cent were rejected and rated unfit for service. However, by the end of December 1942, 32,000 Chinese troops were in training at Ramgarh to create a two-division force (38th and 22nd Chinese Divisions) along with three accompanying artillery regiments and the First Provisional Tank Battalion, albeit the latter under American command with many American NCOs serving in the tanks. Stilwell's target date for his combat offensive in Northern Burma was to be February 1943. However, this date had to be postponed until the autumn of 1943. Parenthetically, the rescheduling of Stilwell's offensive to late 1943 almost caused a cancellation of Wingate's *Operation Longcloth*.

In order to achieve the proper training, Stilwell used American officer and NCO liaison teams alongside Chinese commanders at each level. For both Chinese and American morale, Stilwell himself was often on the rifle range, conducting close inspections and setting an example for his officers and NCOs as to how to teach the Chinese recruit and their officers. Colonel Haydon Boatner, who had Chinese language experience and had served in the US 15th Infantry Regiment at Tientsin, became Chief of Staff of the task force in training and, ultimately, the deputy commander of the *Chih Hui Pu*, or Chinese Army in India.

At Ramgarh, Chinese officers were trained in tactics and reaction under combat conditions, much like that which occurred under Stilwell's tutelage at Fort Benning in the early 1930s. The recruits received hands-on training in the use of rifles, machine-guns, mortars, anti-tank guns and rocket-launchers. Jungle warfare training was also implemented and, for artillery crews, a six-week course in the use of pack artillery and Howitzers, especially under jungle conditions. General Sun Li-jen, a Virginia Military Institute graduate and an evacuee from the fighting in Burma earlier in 1942, maintained command of the 38th Division while General Liao Yao-hsiang, a student of the French military academy at St Cyr, commanded the 22nd Division.

Ramgarh trainees in late 1942, now healthy and outfitted in British khaki drill uniforms, Mk I helmets, the Enfield P-17 rifle and some NCOs having Thompson sub-machine-guns. *(USAMHI)*

An American instructor (*right*) inspects the barrel of his trainee's Enfield P-17 rifle, furnished by the Americans and British but became the standard Chinese infantryman's rifle. (*USAMHI*)

American instructor shows proper method of holding and firing the Thompson sub-machine-gun, which provided devastating volume and spread of fire at short range and had great stopping power. (*USAMHI*)

Lying in prone position, trainees are shown how to fire their Enfield P-17 rifles, which was the product of joint effort by the British and Americans in 1918. (*USAMHI*)

A Chinese soldier practising the stabbing method of a human-sized upper torso replica made of straw-filled burlap with the long sword bayonet fitted to his Enfield P-17 rifle. (*USAMHI*)

Chinese crew of a M1917A1 .30 calibre Browning water-cooled machine gun instructed in posture, aiming and ammunition belt loading. A water container and hose to keep the barrel cool is on ground. (*USAMHI*)

Ammunition belt-loading for the .30 calibre Browning machine-gun, a favourite heavy support defensive weapon with high fire rate that could be disassembled for transport on a mule. *(USAMHI)*

Chinese trainees fire a Bren Mk I gun from tripod. The Bren had a relatively low rate of fire with a 30-round magazine but was highly accurate. *(USAMHI)*

Instructors train Chinese soldiers how to use a 3-inch mortar. Due to limited artillery and tank support, often the mortar was the infantry's heaviest weapon against entrenched Japanese positions. *(USAMHI)*

Chinese troops train with a flamethrower. Tactically, sub-machine-gun fire would suppress Japanese bunkers while a flamethrower worked to get within the 120ft range of this weapon. *(USAMHI)*

Chinese practice with the M9 Bazooka, which fired either a high-explosive or high-explosive anti-tank warhead, making the weapon effective against both bunkers and tanks. (*USAMHI*)

US instructor watches Chinese crew of a 75mm M1-A1 pack Howitzer fire their artillery piece. The average Chinese soldier could be trained to operate this gun in only a week. (*USAMHI*)

This crew fires their pack Howitzer from cover, as they learned from their US instructors how to use the terrain they would encounter in Burma. *(USAMHI)*

Breech of a 75mm pack Howitzer. Most guns supplied to the Chinese were mounted on older carriages with wooden wheels, but the crew were trained to disassemble them for loading onto mules. *(USAMHI)*

Chinese troops learn about the Universal Infantry or Bren carrier, a tracked transport vehicle that could mount a variety of different weapons including Bren gun, Boyes anti-tank rifle or mortar. (*USAMHI*)

M3 light tanks of the 1st Provisional Tank Battalion at Ramgarh, which was under overall command of Col Rothwell Brown and had some mixed crews. (*USAMHI*)

Stilwell (*centre*) observes artillery target practice with his liaison staff officers at Ramgarh. The hard training of the crews would pay off during the stalemate in the Hukawng Valley. (*USAMHI*)

Stilwell (*right*) watches an M3 light tank at Jeep manoeuvre near Ramgarh. He would need the firepower of his 1st Provisional Tank Battalion battling down the Hukawng and Mogaung Valleys. (*USAMHI*)

Stilwell addresses Chinese troops after completion of training at Ramgarh. He was highly visible during all aspects of training and taught his liaison officers to respect the Chinese fighting ability. (*USAMHI*)

Stilwell (*left*) and his deputy, Brig Gen Haydon Boatner (*second from right*), in Burma. Boatner respected his Chinese pupils but had to motivate them when attacking the entrenched Japanese. (*USAMHI*)

Chapter Four

The Chindits and
Operation Longcloth, 1943

For his 77th Indian Brigade, Wingate was given the 13th King's Liverpool regiment as a nucleus of troops. It was an odd choice, since this regiment had been on coastal defence duties in England prior to transfer to India and was to serve primarily as garrison troops and, as such, were considered second-line troops. Ironically, most had lived in large urban centres such as Liverpool and Manchester and the average age was over 30. Many were married while others were physically incompetent for the rigorous training regime Wingate had in store for them. After some serious culling of the ranks, approximately 40 per cent would be weeded out.

The Chindits' 77th Brigade was to be comprised of eight columns originally of 400 men each, which was based on an infantry company's size. However, Column 6 had to be broken up to replace casualties incurred in training among the other seven Columns. Half of the columns were Gurkha, the others British.

Members of the Gurkha Rifles were formed largely of under-age recruits with inexperienced officers and NCOs. The under-strength Burma Rifles were seasoned troops composed of Karens, Kachins and Chins, who also supplied reconnaissance platoons for the other columns. Neither the mules nor the muleteers to lead them were readily available so Wingate elected to have the Gurkhas comprise the majority of the muleteers. However, their performance would become problematic during the operation. Wingate admitted after the operation that 'most of the Gurkhas entered Burma insufficiently trained'. The Sabotage Group, 142 Commando Company was comprised of well-trained demolition experts and survivors of Calvert's Bush Warfare School in Maymyo and were distributed among the columns. Each column was commanded by a major and accompanied by RAF radio operators.

Wingate's new brigade was quartered at Saugor in central India, many miles from the nearest road and located squarely in the jungle. He intended to train his men in jungle warfare under conditions as gruelling as anything they might encounter in the campaign, until every Chindit became a self-reliant, toughened and cunning jungle fighter facile with field craft for survival in order to defeat the Japanese. After the arduous training and further culling of the ranks, the brigade was staged through

Tamu on the Assam-Burma border for their upcoming crossing of the Chindwin River. It was Wingate's tactical construct that each of his columns should march independently with the ability to sustain their trek for one week before radioing the RAF for air resupply.

Furthermore, Wingate espoused that, in principle, a column's security was its mobility and ability to disperse and regroup if confronted by larger enemy forces. However, once the fog of war descended during combat, dispersal frequently resulted in chaos when it proved impossible to brief everyone on the rendezvous to which every man should head. In principle, the absence of wheeled transport and LOC were positive features. However, this made supply by parachute drop an imperative for *Operation Longcloth*. For transport, Wingate would revert to pack animals such as elephants, bullocks and, most importantly, mules. Wingate also postulated that during at least the initial portion of his mission, before reaching the Irrawaddy, the camouflage offered by the jungles and teak forests of northern Burma would be a strong asset.

The Short Magazine Lee-Enfield (SMLE) rifle, Bren gun, Boyes anti-tank rifle, Vickers medium machine gun, Thompson sub-machine gun, and 3- and 6-inch mortars were among the usual infantry weapons utilized by Wingate's force. There was no heavy transport and mules carried the larger equipment. Since air-supply was of paramount importance, an RAF signal section was attached to each column to direct British aircraft to suitable parachute dropping zones, which were always under the threat of Japanese Army fighters based at Myitkyina and other Burmese airfields. The term Chindit now entrenched in military lore, was derived from Wingate misunderstanding the pronunciation of the Burmese word for lion, 'Chinthe', the supreme animal of the Burma jungle.

After months of training for the first Chindit mission, *Operation Longcloth*, a strategic hurdle developed in early February 1943 that almost cancelled it. Wavell had intended to send 77th Brigade into Burma on foot in advance of an assault by 4 Corps from Assam across the Chindwin River into Burma. These British operations were to temporally coincide with two Chinese offensives: one mounted from China's Yunnan province and the other being a Sino-American effort, under General Stilwell, entering Burma south from Ledo in north-east Assam. Wingate's mission was to support these other operations by interfering with Japanese LOC, principally by destroying large portions of the railway to the west of the Irrawadday River. After that, Wingate envisioned 77th Brigade crossing the Irrawaddy to further disrupt the IJA LOC on the Salween River front, where the Chinese forces in Yunnan were to advance.

The Chinese invasions of Burma (including Stilwell's), which were out of Wavell's control, as well as 4 Corps' offensive were all cancelled in early 1943, thereby seeming to force the scuttling of Wingate's *Operation Longcloth* on 3 February. Only the Arakan offensive of 1943 would go on as planned. GHQ in Delhi stipulated that a

Chindit invasion of central Burma alone would fail and would also alert the Japanese to Stilwell's ultimate intentions in Northern Burma. Wavell went to Imphal to discuss the situation with the Chindit leader on 7 February.

Wavell approved the continuation of *Operation Longcloth* to depart from Imphal on 8 February after a spirited debate in which Wingate offered six major points to support his contention as to how his LRP alone could provide a meaningful strategic endpoint:

1. It would be a vital chance to mission- and field-test his ideas.
2. Cancellation would shatter the élan that had developed in 77th Indian Brigade.
3. *Operation Longcloth* would test whether the Burmese would assist the British to evict the Japanese from their country.
4. The Chindit LRP would reduce the pressure of a Japanese offensive on Fort Hertz, the last British bastion in Burma, already underway by the 114th Regiment of Tanaka's 18th IJA Division stationed in Myitkyina.
5. The Chindit operation could disrupt Japanese infiltration across the Chindwin River into India.
6. *Operation Longcloth* might pre-empt any Japanese offensive against Assam in 1943.

Wingate needed *Operation Longcloth* to validate his military theories, which were on a much larger scale than those in the Sudan, Palestine or Ethiopia. As an aside, in Burma there would be no political cause for Wingate to champion as he had earlier in the Middle East.

Wingate's main body (Northern Group) crossed the Chindwin River, just over the India-Burma border, on 13 February at Tonhe, where the river was only 400 yards wide. The diversionary force of two columns, under the command of Lieutenant Colonel Leigh Alexander (Southern Group), did so 50 miles to the south near Auktaung. Its intent was to draw attention away from the main effort in the north, and 77th Brigade was never discovered by the Japanese crossing the Chindwin. Their task was to attack Japanese outposts, cut railway lines and blow up bridges.

The Southern Group attacked the Mandalay-Myitkyina railway at Kyaikthin, some 200km (125 miles) north of Mandalay, in early March after making the first encounter with a small Japanese force at Maingnyaung on 18 February. After losing many pack animals, which produced a delay of three days, this group moved eastwards again. Despite Wingate's secrecy, the Japanese had uncovered the Chindits' order of battle following an inadvertent air drop and drew in their patrols eastward and evacuated all outposts to concentrate more centrally.

Wingate and the Northern Group's five columns also aimed to strike the same railway line between Wuntho and Indaw, farther to the north. Major Fergusson's

No. 5 Column and Major Calvert's No. 3 Column destroyed the railway and some bridges in over seventy places on 6 March. This section of the railway wound through the middle of Northern Burma providing the IJA with an excellent LOC for supply and reinforcement in an inhospitable terrain. Despite this demolition the Japanese, with the help of forced labour, restored the railway line within four weeks. Although these attacks took the Japanese by surprise, they recovered quickly and began closing in. Many small but ferocious actions were fought. Two columns were forced to disperse and make their perilous trip back to India as best they could.

The specific operational dilemma for Wingate was whether crossing the Irrawaddy was more hazardous than taking his depleted columns in a reverse course through jungle country, which was now teeming with Japanese patrols. Wingate signalled Calvert and Fergusson from his HQ area north of Wuntho in the Bambwe Taung Hills asking them if they considered it more prudent to retire to the mountains above Wuntho to form a redoubt, or to go on eastwards across the river. Both agreed to cross the Irrawaddy without delay.

Finally, it must be stated that when Wavell re-approved *Operation Longcloth*, his orders specifically provided for 77th Brigade's crossing of the Irrawaddy as long as it appeared possible, in order to evaluate and test the limits of LRP. Numbers 3 and 5 Columns led the way across the Irrawaddy River with Calvert's group ordered to blow up the Gokteik Gorge viaduct, which carried the Lashio Road about 100km (60 miles) north of Mandalay. Wingate and the rest of his force followed. Now the columns had to cross a triangular area between the Irrawaddy and Shweli rivers. To their dismay, related to poor reconnaissance, they found it to be open, waterless country, bisected by roads and tracks along which Japanese tanks and armoured cars patrolled. Also, the Chindits were at the extreme end of RAF air resupply. For guerrilla operations this situation had the makings of a disaster.

On 24 March Wingate was instructed, and complied with an order, to re-cross the Irrawaddy and commence a withdrawal to the Chindwin, which with the IJA presence on the west bank of the river and only a few boats made this prospect a daunting one. Ultimately, dispersal of the still extant columns into smaller groups was needed and carried out. The next day, with his remaining men weak from hunger, exhaustion and disease, Wingate ordered them to try to get back to India in small independent groups. The wounded had to be abandoned. Of the original 3,000, 2,182 returned, over 800 were lost, killed, wounded or captured, many as they re-crossed the Chindwin, where Japanese patrols awaited them. Only 600 were ever fit enough to fight again. Was the sacrifice of about 30 per cent of the force worthwhile? In material terms, little was achieved when some railway lines were cut and a few hundred Japanese killed. But in terms of morale, their achievements were incalculable. In a small brigade-sized operation, spanning over six weeks, the myth of Japanese invincibility had been exposed as well as some of Wingate's theories and training methods being proven for subsequent missions. The Chindits had taken on the Japanese man-for-man in the jungle and although battered, starving and disease-ridden, had beaten him and returned to India with their accounts imbuing a new spirit among the defeat-ridden Indian Army. Heroes were sorely needed and Wingate was lionized in the press and summoned by Churchill to the Quebec Conference of Allied leaders in August 1943, where he won approval for an expanded second Chindit operation and a more ambitious expedition in co-operation with the Chinese and the Americans.

A Chindit's trek through the dense, hot, humid jungle was accompanied by torrential rain, deep mud, bamboo thickets, leeches, ants, spiders and other predatory animals. Many Chindits wore beards making a shaving kit unnecessary, and also protecting the facial skin from mosquitoes and ticks. A typical day's march would start just before dawn and was divided into one-hour stages. Each soldier carried a pack weighing about 27kg (60lb), while pack mules carried supplies. Rations were less than 1kg (about 2lb) per day, consisting of biscuits, cheese, nuts and raisins, dates, tea, sugar, milk and chocolate. These were sometimes supplemented by rice, bananas and other fruit from friendly villagers. Some supplies were dropped by air, but this became more difficult when the columns had to disperse. Wingate demonstrated that despite the adversities, his British infantryman could overcome the jungle's inclement conditions and successfully combat the vaunted Japanese soldier.

Wavell (*centre*) discusses aspects of the upcoming *Operation Longcloth* with Wingate (*far right*) and Fergusson (*to Wavell's right*), who commanded Column 5 in the first LRP into Burma in 1943. (*Author's collection*)

Wingate's Gurkha Rifles were insufficiently trained, underage recruits who had six months of gruelling jungle training in the sweltering heat and torrential rain of India's Central Provinces' monsoon season. (*USAMHI*)

(*Above*) A C-47 parachutes supplies to waiting Chindits near lit signal flares east of the Irrawaddy, which was approaching the end of the RAF's range for continued supplies. (*USAMHI*)

(*Opposite above*) Chindits use dugouts for river crossings in India. Vessels of all types were necessary for Burma's rivers the Chindits would have to cross, often under combat conditions, during *Operation Longcloth*. (*USAMHI*)

(*Opposite below*) A group of Chindits ferried across the Chindwin River early during *Operation Longcloth* after their arduous training in India's jungles and culling of the ranks. (*USAMHI*)

(*Above*) A securely tied British aircrew pushes and kicks out supplies for the Chindits in the Burmese jungle below. Static lines tripped the parachutes to open once out of the transport's cabin. (*USAMHI*)

(*Opposite above*) Commonwealth airmen on alert at their Vickers machine-guns on a supply run during *Operation Longcloth* since Japanese fighter interdiction was always a threat with or without RAF fighter escort. (*USAMHI*)

(*Opposite below*) The American-built RAF Vultee Vengence returns to Assam after a dive-bombing sortie in close support of British troops against the Japanese in the Burmese jungle in the spring of 1943. (*Nat. Arch. RG-208-AA-11B-2*)

(*Above*) Chindits await an airdrop during *Longcloth*. Crossing to the Irrawaddy's eastern bank was putting the Chindits out of range for RAF resupply of rations, animal feed and ammunition. (*USAMHI*)

(*Opposite above*) The venerable Hawker Hurricane spent its last days as a fighter/ground attack bomber in Burma in 1943. Although unwieldy against the *Oscar*, its twelve machine-guns were effective against bombers. (*USAMHI*)

(*Opposite below*) Chindits return to a Kachin village with airdropped supplies. RAF and American aircrew that flew those missions had to contend with all types of terrain to make their drops. (*USAMHI*).

Gurkhas comprised the majority of the Chindit muleteers during *Longcloth*. However, many mules were lost due to their combat inexperience after an early skirmish at Maingnyaung on 18 February. (*USAMHI*)

Chindit column crosses a river with full packs. Weapon, personal clothing and equipment, ammunition, water container, haversack, machete, rations, mess tin, and blanket could often reach 50–70lb per man. (*USAMHI*)

For proximate patrolling away from their camped column, a Chindit section marches single-file with only their personal weapons and ammunition pouches. (*USAMHI*)

Calvert's Column 3 place charges to destroy a railway bridge at Nankan on 6 March. Truck-borne Japanese from Wuntho were ambushed by other Chindits, enabling the demolitions to be detonated. (*Author's collection*)

Column 5 leader Major Fergusson (*far left*) talks to Kachin headman (*right background*) with other column members (*l-to-r*) Lieutenant Harman, Corporal Dorans and Captain Fraser. Village huts are in background. (*USAMHI*)

Chindits wave farewell to a photography crew flying out of Burma in an L5, aware they would walk 170 miles to India on the return trip during *Operation Longcloth*. (*USAMHI*)

(*l-to-r*) Wavell, Stilwell, Gen Henry Arnold, Lt Gen Brehon Somervell and Gen Sir John Dill at New Delhi, 1943, to discuss the implications of *Operation Longcloth* for future Burma missions. (*USAMHI*)

Chapter Five

Office of Strategic Services (OSS) Detachment 101 and Kachin Rangers

In April 1942 William Donovan, Roosevelt's appointee as Co-ordinator of Information (a forerunner of the Office of Strategic Services or OSS) prepared the necessary groundwork in Burma for activation of Detachment 101 to work behind enemy lines gathering intelligence, ambushing Japanese columns through guerrilla actions, identifying bombing targets for the USAAF and to rescue downed Allied airmen. Detachment 101, never more than a few hundred Americans, relied on its manpower from various Burmese tribal groups but, in particular, the Kachins. These tribesmen were virulently anti-Japanese, which stemmed from their loyalty to Westerners from their pre-war relationship with Christian missionaries and doctors who cared for them.

In February 1942 Stilwell approved of the Co-ordinator of Information to form Detachment 101 and proposed Carl Eifler, a former US Treasury agent who had also served as a lieutenant in a reserve unit Stilwell once commanded, to be the first commanding officer with a rank of captain. Eifler was given the authority to pick anyone he wanted for his new unit and he selected Captain John Coughlin, a West Point graduate, to be his deputy. Coughlin then recruited Captain William R. Peers and this triumvirate recruited, trained and equipped the original contingent of Detachment 101.

Eifler's charge from Stilwell in Northern Burma was to deny the use of the Myitkyina airfield by Japanese fighters. Also, he was to organize Kachin tribesmen, loyal to the Allies, to conduct sabotage of railroads, bridges and river tankers as well as set up ambushes on Japanese troop detachments, in between Myitkyina and Fort Hertz to the north. Stilwell also wanted the officers and men of Detachment 101 to learn how to survive and live in the jungles. The British were co-operative in making available potential agents found among the Burmese nationals in the Indian Army. Other potential agents were found in refugee camps. Much of what Detachment 101 did was completely novel and learned via trial and error.

In July 1942 twenty OSS men set up their headquarters in north-eastern Assam. Starting in 1943, small groups of OSS from the Nazira base camp in India were parachuted to remote Kachin villages well-behind the enemy's lines and resupply was conducted by parachute drop. These American OSS officers infiltrated Burma in January 1943 to report intelligence, carry out sabotage and guide Allied bombers to Japanese targets. Later, bases were established from which L5 liaison planes could bring in other personnel and evacuate the wounded. It was from these bases that the OSS officers recruited the Kachins of Northern Burma.

In December 1943 Stilwell issued a directive that Detachment 101 should be augmented to 3,000 Kachins. The Kachin Rangers possessed great jungle skills, harboured intense animus towards the Japanese, and quickly learned how to use radios for effective communication to co-ordinate their myriad activities. At Fort Hertz in the north, British officers had commanded a battalion of mountain tribesmen called the Northern Kachin Levies. During Stilwell's Myitkyina offensive across the Kumon Range, and ultimately against the airfield at Myitkyina in the spring of 1944, Detachment 101, with their 600 Kachin Rangers, scouted ahead of Merrill's Marauders and provided flank protection while also attacking Japanese LOC.

Upon its deactivation in July 1945, Detachment 101 had killed 5,428 Japanese and rescued Allied airmen for a total of approximately thirty Americans and 338 Kachins killed. An additional 10,000 Japanese soldiers were wounded by this group's activities and seventy-eight were taken prisoner. It cannot be emphasized enough that Detachment 101's efforts screened the advances for the larger Allied three-principal offensive forces in Northern Burma: Stilwell's Chinese forces, Wingate's Chindits and Merrill's Marauders' envelopments and their assault on the Myitkyina airfield, in addition to their own activities at severing Japanese LOC.

Kachin Rangers at inspection with a variety of weapons and wearing mixed local garb and uniform, which helped for infiltrating enemy lines and aid distinguishing themselves from the Japanese. (*Nat. Arch. 111-SC-199224-S*)

Kachin Rangers in a trench. Ranger (*foreground*) is armed with an M3 machine pistol called a grease gun, while the one seated next to him has a British SMLE rifle. (*USAMHI*)

Two Kachin Rangers, one locally-garbed and the other in uniform (*far right*) who points with a bamboo rod at some map features examined by three American OSS officers. (*USAMHI*)

Kachin Rangers adept at reconnaissance, fire discipline and ambush technique are armed with SMLE rifles and a Bren light machine-gun while awaiting a Japanese column. (*Nat. Arch. 111-SC-37121-FO*)

Kachin Rangers armed with a Thompson sub-machine-gun and SMLE rifles lie in ambush against the Japanese. They destroyed the enemy's LOC and garrisons throughout Northern Burma. *(Nat. Arch. F-45-0050)*

Kachin Rangers fire a Browning air-cooled .30 calibre heavy machine-gun. The 14lb tripod made it double a Bren gun's weight requiring three men to carry it and ammunition. *(Nat. Arch. 111-SC-199220-S)*

A group of Kachin Rangers wearing a mixture of military uniforms, south of Myitkyina in 1944. Local native porters (*left*) indicate the group's proximity to an airdrop. (*USAMHI*)

Two American OSS officers with their Kachin Rangers lie in a jungle clearing after detecting an approaching Japanese column. (*USAMHI*)

(*Above*) A C-46 transport completes air resupply for Detachment 101 OSS personnel north of Myitkyina in 1944. A local Burmese assists in the ferrying of the Americans with their new supplies. (*USAMHI*)

(*Opposite above*) American OSS officer (*right*) points out map features to his Kachin Rangers. These Kachins are armed with the M1 Garand carbine, which was better-suited to their smaller stature. (*USAMHI*)

(*Opposite below*) Kachin villagers disdainful of the Japanese march with a Marauder column in Northern Burma. A task of the OSS was to generate unfavourable propaganda towards the Japanese for native consumption. (*Nat. Arch. RG-208-AA-S99062*)

(*Above*) The Kachins showed their loyalty to the Allies on the battlefield and in their villages. A locally made poster reads: 'The Japanese invasions will absolutely be bitten by the strong armed Allies.' (*USAMHI*)

(*Opposite above*) Kachin villager gives a chicken to Brigadier Merrill. Fr James Steward, an Irish missionary in Burma for eight years, also sits on the bench. (*Nat. Arch. RG-208-AA-R-7*)

(*Opposite below*) OSS NCOs on either side of a Kachin Ranger patrol leader ford a shallow stream in Northern Burma on mission to disrupt Japanese LOC and ambush their columns. (*USAMHI*)

An OSS detachment in Northern Burma displays captured Japanese battle flags. They and their Kachin Rangers accounted for over 5,000 Japanese dead and over 10,000 wounded Japanese soldiers. (*USAMHI*)

Chapter Six

Fighting in the Hukawng Valley, 1943–1944

Stilwell's Northern Burma Campaign was re-established to begin on 1 December 1943 after the earlier cancellation in February 1943. However, elements of the 38th Chinese Division had received orders in October 1943 to move forward into Burma to cover the onward movement of the Ledo Road and reach the Tarung River, which was the starting point for Stilwell's offensive in the Hukawng Valley. The Tarung River flows from north to south and enters the westward-flowing Tanai River about 6 miles south-west of the village of Yupbang Ga. These two rivers lay in the path of the engineers building the Ledo Road so it was essential for Stilwell to control their crossings.

The three battalions of the 112th Regiment, Chinese 38th Division were sent into the northern Hukawng Valley by Stilwell to seize the two river crossings from the Japanese garrisons there. However, elements of the Chinese 112th Regiment moved forward and clashed with a reconnaissance company of the IJA 18th Division, under the overall command of Lieutenant General Shinichi Tanaka, on 30 October 1943. Tanaka had deployed the 55th and 56th regiments of his division to the Hukawng Valley, while he kept his third regiment, the 114th, stationed at Myitkyina. After Mutaguchi decided in September 1943 to launch *Operation U-Go* against General Slim in Assam in March 1944, Tanaka knew that he would not receive any reinforcements in the Hukawng Valley. Tanaka regarded the Hukawng Valley as an awful place, with its name meaning 'Valley of Death'. From 15 to 50 miles across, east to west, it extended north to south for 130 miles, was transected by many rivers and was easily turned into a marshy quagmire by the monsoon, so creating a nest for cholera and malaria. Tanaka had no wish to commit all of his 18th Division to this hellhole, so he sent only Colonel Nagahisa's 56th Regiment north to face the Chinese 38th Division under General Sun Li-Jen.

By early November the Chinese had encountered Nagahisa's well-led and well-entrenched 56th Regiment at Yupbang Ga, a crossing-point on the Tarung River before it feeds into the Tanai River. As a result of the Japanese enveloping jungle tactics, the three Chinese battalions of the 112th Regiment became surrounded with one of the Chinese companies being completely destroyed by Nagahisa's men. This necessitated Brigadier General Boatner, Stilwell's deputy and Chief of Staff for the Chinese Army in India, to send in the remainder of the Chinese 38th Division by the end of November 1943 to help extricate the remnants of the isolated 112th Regiment's three battalions from the Japanese encirclements. Until then the Chinese had been relying on air supply to sustain themselves with rations and ammunition.

Stilwell arrived at his forward echelon headquarters at Shingbwiyang, in the Hukawng Valley, on 21 December 1943 with his offensive already a month late. He observed first-hand that the Japanese at Yupbang Ga had isolated the 112th Regiment of 38th Chinese Division, with relief attempts having already failed, and lambasted his Chinese officers while he also arranged for a co-ordinated attack, exhorting the troops that they must succeed, which seemed to work. From 24 December it took a week of intense fighting at extremely close quarters, with Stilwell directly supervising an artillery barrage, to clear the Japanese out of their entrenched positions at Yupbang Ga, costing 38th Division 315 killed and 429 wounded but providing the Chinese with their first victory in Burma over the Japanese.

Tanaka was enraged but also impressed by the fighting quality of the Chinese soldier in Burma coupled with an awesome display of air resupply to Allied ground forces. True to his aggressive zeal, Tanaka decided to make an advance right up the Hukawng to Shingbwiyang, Stilwell's advanced headquarters, but Mutaguchi would not permit an offensive that might divert supplies or motor support from his upcoming Imphal offensive, *Operation U-Go*, and told him to hold Maingkwan, to the south-east in the centre of the valley. Stilwell's 38th and now 22nd Chinese divisions moved slowly down the Hukawng, and came to a halt on 29 January 1944. Stilwell was going to have to change his tactics to descend the Hukawng Valley at a faster rate in order to get to Myitkyina before the monsoon season arrived. Tanaka was already planning that by the time the rains fell in May or June, he would have created a stalemate near the Jambu Bum ridgeline, which separates the southern end of the Hukawng Valley from the Mogaung Valley, and where he had 75mm mountain guns and 150mm Howitzers.

IJA Fifteenth Army commander General Mutaguchi (*centre seated*), has to his right Lt Gen Shinichi Tanaka, who took over command of the IJA 18th Division from the former. (*USAMHI*)

Chinese 38th Division infantry pass Ledo Road US Army Engineers to enter the Hukawng Valley in October 1943. They would soon meet entrenched Japanese troops. (*USAMHI*)

(*Above*) Chinese troops construct a pontoon bridge of shallow draft boats across one of the many river crossings in the Hukawng Valley. (*USAMHI*)

(*Opposite above*) Chinese artillery train moving pack Howitzers and ammunition through the jungle using mules for transport. Artillery support was vital to victory at Yupbang Ga. (*Nat. Arch. 111-SC-266098*)

(*Opposite below*) Chinese troops haul a 75mm pack Howitzer with wooden wheels into position near Yupbang Ga to support their surrounded infantry there. (*Nat. Arch. RG-208-AA-16717-PME*)

Chinese 105mm Howitzer gun crew of the 38th Division fires on Japanese positions. Heavy weaponry was required to destroy the bamboo-fortified Japanese bunkers at Yupbang Ga. (Nat. Arch. 111-SC-262509)

Chinese troops attacking through wooded terrain under cover of an artillery barrage. The soldier in the foreground is carrying a Bren light machine-gun. (Nat. Arch. 111-SC-197903-9)

Chinese troops providing direct fire-support with a water-cooled Browning .30 calibre M1917 Heavy Machine-Gun with a river bank in the background. (*USAMHI*)

Chinese 6-inch mortar crew sets up their weapon in the open adjacent to dense jungle behind them. High explosive rounds from these weapons might not destroy Japanese fortified bunkers. (*USAMHI*)

M3 light tanks of the First Provisional Chinese Tank Battalion ford a shallow stream. Upon being isolated at Yupbang Ga, the armour was supplied by airdrop. (*USAMHI*)

An American transport aircrew is about to push and kick out supplies to Chinese troops below isolated by the Japanese in the Hukawng Valley. (*USAMHI*)

Isolated Chinese troops at Yupbang Ga open up supplies that were parachuted into their defensive box by American C-47 and C-46 transport aircraft. *(USAMHI)*

Chinese 37mm anti-tank gun crew deploys and readies their weapon against light Japanese armour in the Hukawng Valley. (*USAMHI*)

Rear view of a disabled Type 95 *Ha-Go* Japanese light tank used primarily for infantry support. Their thin armour made them an easy target for Allied tanks and anti-tank guns. (*USAMHI*)

A dead Japanese soldier lies outside his bunker, which had its earthen roof reinforced with wood planking to make it impervious to small arms and light artillery fire. (*USAMHI*)

(*Above*) A Chinese patrol casually inspects the bodies of recently killed Japanese by a road traversing thick woods and vegetation. (*USAMHI*)

(*Opposite above*) Two Chinese soldiers fighting in jungle near the opening to a deserted Japanese sniper hole. The two have different uniforms, which was not uncommon. (*Nat. Arch. 111-SC-266086*)

(*Opposite below*) Chinese horse-laden supply train passes Japanese corpses at side of road. Noses and mouths covered due to the stench of the enemy dead. (*USAMHI*)

(*Above*) A captured Japanese soldier of the 18th Division holds on to his mess cup. He was taken prisoner near Lakyan Ga in the Hukawng Valley. (*Nat. Arch. 111-SC-263240*)

(*Opposite above*) Three barefoot Japanese prisoners are blindfolded and led away by their Chinese captors down a grass-covered road near wooded terrain. (*Nat. Arch. CAN 711917WP*)

(*Opposite below*) A Japanese prisoner is interrogated by a Chinese officer and his American liaison counterpart writes notes while under the guard of a Chinese soldier with Thompson sub-machine gun. (*USAMHI*)

Wounded Chinese soldier lying on his side is attended to by two medical personnel while others lie on mats and mattresses at the roadside. (*USAMHI*)

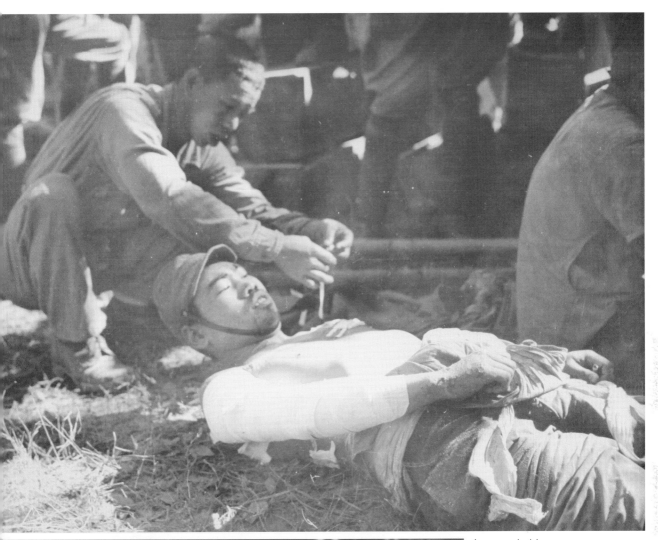

A wounded Japanese prisoner receives aid from a Chinese medical orderly after being captured in one of the numerous fire-fights in the Hukawng Valley. (*USAMHI*)

Colonel Rothwell Brown, the American officer-in-charge of the First Provisional Tank Battalion, congratulates his Chinese troops after victory over the Japanese in the Hukawng Valley. (*USAMHI*)

(*Above*) Chinese troops of the 1/114, 38th Division, cross the Taihpa Ga River as they descend the Hukawng Valley after earlier victories. (*Nat. Arch. 111 SC-263238*)

(*Opposite above*) Gen Sun Li-jen commander of the 38th Chinese Division (*left*), Stilwell, and Lt Gen Liao Yao-hsiang commander of the 22nd Division go over map coordinates in the Hukawng Valley. (*USAMHI*)

(*Opposite below*) American Major Batachelor, an Infantry liaison officer, eating with Chinese officers at their HQ near Mungwam in the Hukawng Valley 2 March 1944. (*Nat. Arch. III-SC-263246*)

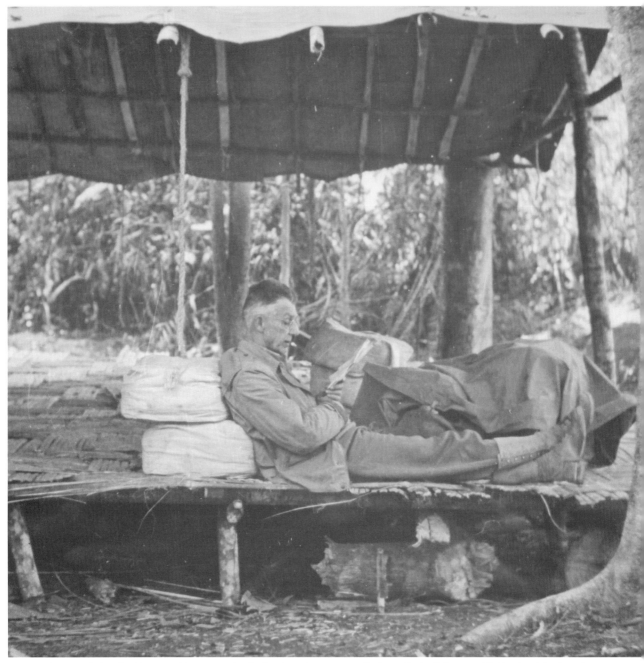

General Stilwell relaxes at his forward echelon headquarters at Taihpa Ga in February 1944 after his victories over General Tanaka's 18th Division in the upper Hukawng Valley. (*Nat. Arch. 111-SC-263235*)

Chapter Seven

Merrill's Marauders and Stilwell's Envelopments

On 4 February Stilwell planned to put his sole US infantry unit, the 5307th Composite Unit (Provisional), codenamed *GALAHAD*, to effect deep envelopments or 'hooks' around Tanaka's right flank to ultimately block the Kamaing Road while his 22nd and 38th Chinese Divisions, plus the 1st Provisional Tank Battalion, pushed down from the north to isolate elements of the 18th IJA Division in the Hukawng and Mogaung Valleys. In essence, Stilwell would be continually and simultaneously attacking the enemy on two fronts and if Tanaka had to retreat, his exit would be blocked by *GALAHAD*. American newspapermen, who had marched with *GALAHAD* from Ledo to Shingbwiyang, renamed the unit 'Merrill's Marauders' after Brigadier General Frank Merrill, who had taken over command in early January 1944.

The Marauders' training camp, under Wingate's direct supervision, was located on the Betwa River near the small village of Deogarh in central India. Deogarh was about 20 miles south of Lallitpur, the Chindits' training camp. It was their home for nine weeks until they left for Burma at the end of January 1944. This isolated and desolate area had been picked by Brigadier General Orde Wingate, under whose command the Marauders were supposed to fight in Burma, and built by the British for the American volunteer force. The groundcover in the desolate plateau at Deogarh was completely different from the rain forest of Burma. At Deogarh it was steamy hot during the day and cold at night. The training there was typical for Wingate's indoctrination, namely forced marches and extensive practice with all of the infantry weapons that would be carried into Burma.

Originally, *GALAHAD* was under Mountbatten's operational control and Wingate's training command at the Deogarh camp and was to furnish three LRP groups to operate under Wingate and go in during the dry season in 1944 into Northern Burma. However, Stilwell pestered Mountbatten for American ground forces and ultimately Mountbatten transferred operational command to Stilwell's Northern Combat Area Command (NCAC) under the direct command of Brigadier General Frank Merrill. The Marauders, like the Chindits, had no heavy artillery or tanks but they were effectively organized for Stilwell's particular spearheading role, with special sections for pioneer, demolition, intelligence and reconnaissance work. Their weapons included M1 carbines, sub-machine-guns, light and heavy machine guns, mortars and rocket launchers. These weapons and the ammunition meant that each combat team needed a large number of mules. Merrill used his knowledge of Japanese to gain maximum benefit from the Nisei, the Japanese-speaking Americans who were used for all aspects of intelligence work.

For Stilwell an envelopment, or hook, was to surprise the enemy in the rear by circling his flank through almost impassable mountain jungles. In February 1944 the Marauders received their orders for their first envelopment to be at Walawbum in the southern Hukawng Valley, with the second one south of the Jambu Bum in the vicinity of both Shaduzup and Inkangahtawng in the Mogaung Valley. From 23 February until 4 March 1944, Stilwell started his advance. In this, their combat debut, the Marauders swept widely to the eastern side of the Hukawng Valley, in order to hinder Tanaka's 18th Division retreat southwards. In close support of the Marauders' hook, the 22nd Chinese Division with the 1st Provisional Chinese Tank Battalion of sixty light tanks under the American command of Colonel Brown advanced on 3 March down a road towards Maingkwan and Walawbum to the south-east.

The battle raged for five days from 4–8 March 1944, after which Tanaka, having suffered over 800 Japanese dead to only eight Marauders killed, disengaged and headed west and south away from Walawbum to attempt to pick up the Kamaing Road in the Mogaung Valley. The retreat of the Japanese was all part of the main attack that Stilwell did not deviate from. However, his hopes of trapping the whole of General Tanaka's 18th Division were not realized even though the hook by Merrill's Marauders and the southern advance of the Chinese 38th and 22nd divisions had cleared the upper Hukawng Valley. It seems that American intelligence failed to appreciate a secret trail that Tanaka used to extricate his surviving troops and thereby bypass the Marauders. On 15 March, Tanaka dug in on the Jambu Bum at the southern end of the Hukawng Valley with its artillery on the ridgeline.

Towards the end of March 1944, Stilwell chose to employ another envelopment in the Mogaung Valley that had both a short and a long hook. For the short hook, the Marauders' 1st Battalion, led by Colonel William Osborne, along with the Chinese 113th Regiment, insinuated itself stealthily during the night of 27/28 March and attacked south of Shaduzup at dawn. The Marauders overran a Japanese camp, set up a roadblock on the Kamaing Road and held it against counter-attacks until Chinese infantry with pack artillery relieved them.

The 2nd and 3rd Marauder battalions conducted the long hook of the March 1944 envelopment down the east side of the Hukawng Valley to trap Tanaka's 18th Division. From 15–21 March, these two battalions moved through the Kumon hills and on 23 March arrived further south of Shaduzup on the Kamaing Road at the village of Inkangahtawng. It was Stilwell's intent that by placing his Marauders well to the south of Shaduzup he could seal off the entrance to Mogaung Valley and effectively prohibit overland supply, thereby producing a severance of the Japanese 18th Division's Headquarters at Myitkyina in the Irrawaddy Valley from the northernmost Hukawng Valley. The Japanese, under Tanaka, also realized the significance of Stilwell's attacks and were determined to prevent him from reaching Kamaing to the south-west of Inkangahtawng.

Tanaka was aware that if Stilwell captured the town of Kamaing, he would be a potential threat to the upcoming Japanese Fifteenth Army assault on the British garrison at Imphal, *Operation U-Go*, as well as to his own 18th Division's LOC. Elements of the 2nd and 3rd battalions of the Marauders encountered the IJA on 23 March in company strength and dug in at Inkangahtawng. The next day, 24 March, two reinforced Marauder platoons, which were dispatched to surround Inkangahtawng, had to withdraw after finding it too strongly defended. Japanese reinforcements were hastily dispatched to the south from the 18th Division's headquarters at Shaduzup. On 26 March, the Marauders 2nd and 3rd Battalions, both under Colonel Charles N. Hunter's command, learned from Merrill that about two additional understrength battalions of roughly 800 Japanese troops of Tanaka's 114th Regiment were moving north-east from Kamaing towards Nhpum Ga to protect Tanaka's right flank and perhaps isolate the Marauders as they moved east from Inkangahtawng. By 24 March, Tanaka began his attack on the retreating Marauders' 2nd Battalion with a 1,600-man force (comprised of elements of his 55th and 114th regiments) to get around Stilwell's flank as well as capture and then defend Nhpum Ga which, located astride a ridgeline of the Kumon Range, was desirable terrain in the eyes of the Japanese general. However, Merrill too recognized the value of Nhpum Ga and decided that it must be held by the Marauders. Fighting rear-guard actions against this IJA force from Kamaing, the Marauders delayed the Japanese movement toward Nhpum Ga from 26–28 March.

On 30 March the Japanese attacked Nhpum Ga in force. A Japanese detachment led by the 114th Regiment's commanding officer, Colonel Maruyama, took a water-point from the Marauders. Finally on 6 April, only limited water resupply of 2nd Battalion was accomplished causing the battalion's senior surgeon to note, 'Question of drinking or using water for casts.' The 2nd Marauder Battalion lived a day-to-day existence with air resupply their only source of relief.

On 9 April the 3rd Battalion broke through ending the siege of Nhpum Ga. General Merrill wrote later, 'At Nhpum Ga the best part of 3 Jap Bns were engaged. It was a Jap defeat as they withdrew all the way to Myitkyina.'

General Tanaka, becoming more concerned about holding Myitkyina now, did not want to lose any more troops fighting a Marauder defensive position in the hills north-east of Kamaing. The Marauders lost fifty-nine killed and 379 were evacuated (including Merrill with another heart attack) with wounds or sickness while Tanaka's 18th Division lost at least 400 irreplaceable men with the 114th Regiment returning to Myitkyina intact but badly battered.

(*Above*) Col Francis Brink, leader of the 5307th Composite Unit (Provisional), at Deogarh, had experience in jungle warfare and admired Wingate and his methods. Lt Col Charles Hunter oversaw the administration. (*USAMHI*)

(*Opposite above*) The Marauder training camp, under the direction of Wingate, at Deogarh, India in December 1943. The 5307th Composite Unit (Provisional) was originally intended to be a Chindit formation. (*Nat. Arch. 111-SC-277372*)

(*Opposite below*) Wingate (*centre*) converses with Lt Col Charles Beach (*on his left*) after inspection of his 3rd Bn at Deogarh, India. To Beach's left is Brink, on Wingate's right is Hunter. (*USAMHI*)

Admiral Lord Mountbatten, head of SEAC, addresses a group from the 5307th Composite Unit (Provisional) at their Deogarh base in India, where Wingate supervised their training. (USAMHI)

A Marauder fires his M1 Garand rifle in the prone position wearing a full pack in a training exercise at the Deogarh base in early January 1944. (Nat. Arch. 111-SC-277379)

Stilwell (*centre*), Brig Merrill (*left*) and a junior officer at a forward base in Burma. Stilwell had negligible contact with the Marauders during their training or early days in Burma. (*Nat. Arch. 111-SC-263274*)

Marauders hike over the Patkai Mountains during their 110-mile trek from Ledo to Stilwell's forward military base of Shingbwiyang in Burma's Hukawng Valley in February 1944. (*USAMHI*)

Brig Gen Frank Merrill (*left*) watches as the Marauders parade by at the start of their 110-mile trek from Ledo to Shingbwiyang in early February 1944. (*USAMHI*)

Marauders march along a jungle path and pass Kachin villagers on the way to Walawbum in late February 1944. The loyal Kachins would often warn of nearby Japanese patrols. *(USAMHI)*

Alert and on the lookout for the enemy, a Marauder column passes through a desolate Burmese village near Walawbum in late February 1944. *(USAMHI)*

197486-S

(*Above*) Marauders cross a stream on a bamboo bridge single-file while their pack-animals wait on the rear shore as their enveloping march to Walawbum continues in early March 1944. (*Nat. Arch. 111-SC-263252*)

(*Opposite page*) Marauders cross a shallow river with their heavily-laden mules as they descend the Hukawng Valley on their envelopment of the Japanese at Walawbum in early March 1944. (*USAMHI*)

A Marauder patrol marches through the Hukawng Valley's tall jungle brush during their envelopment against the 18th IJA Division at Walawbum on 24 February 1944. (USAMHI)

Weary Marauders and their supply-loaded animals march through a desolate Walawbum after their battle with elements of Tanaka's 55th and 56th Regiments on 4 March 1944. (USAMHI)

Marauders receive dressing changes at a jungle aid station near Walawbum. In addition to battle wounds, skin lesions abounded, notably the Naga sores from infected leech remnants. (*Nat. Arch. 208-AA-11GG-22*)

A Marauder 81mm mortar crew sets up in the jungle outside Walawbum. As members site the weapon, another crewman brings up the mortar rounds. (*USAMHI*)

Marching through tall elephant grass with full packs on, a column of Marauders pass Japanese dead on the jungle track near Walawbum in March 1944. *(USAMHI)*

A Marauder without his field pack but with his M1 Garand carbine at the ready examines a Japanese foxhole hideout for the enemy at Walawbum. (*USAMHI*)

A column of Chinese soldiers of General Sun's 38th Division relieves a Marauder group marching in the opposite direction at Walawbum. *(USAMHI)*

Marauders and Chinese soldiers get first aid in the back of a truck after a friendly-fire occurrence at Walawbum. Fire discipline was a frequent problem among Stilwell's Chinese soldiers. *(USAMHI)*

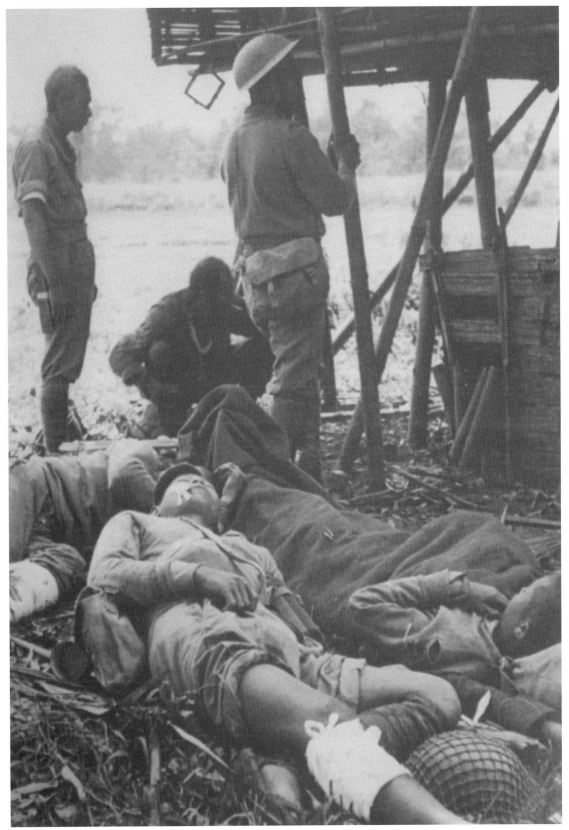

Chinese soldiers and some 1st Bn Marauders had a friendly-fire episode at the fighting's end at Walawbum. Here some Chinese wounded get aid at a makeshift field station. (*USAMHI*)

An American liaison officer confers with two Chinese soldiers near a recently disabled Japanese tank at Walawbum. The Chinese First Provisional Tank Battalion won Stilwell's commendation for their action. *(USAMHI)*

Chinese 38th Division soldiers inspect a captured Japanese tank with 37mm gun buried hull down for the defence of Walawbum. Thin armour made the Japanese tanks inviting targets. (*USAMHI*)

An M3 light tank of the Chinese 1st Provisional Tank Battalion drives down jungle track after engaging Japanese mortar and artillery fire all night 4 March 1944 at Walawbum. (*Nat. Arch. 111-SC-263248*)

(*Above*) A Chinese 105mm Howitzer crew of the 38th Division fires at Japanese positions near Walawbum. Stilwell had high regard for his Chinese artillerymen who were Ramgarh-trained. (*Nat. Arch. 111-SC-30222-FA*)

(*Opposite page*) Chinese troops march single-file down the Kamaing Road with their pack animals on their way to relieve the Marauders at Walawbum in March 1944. (*USAMHI*)

(*Below*) American Signal Corps troops march south down Kamaing Road with Chinese 64th Regiment soldiers near Inkangahtawng. Monsoon rains have not yet turned the road into a quagmire. (*Nat. Arch. 111-SC-266070*)

(*Above*) At Nhpum Ga thirst was a concern for the Marauders who refill their canteens at a jungle stream, a source for dysentery, which like battle casualties would winnow their ranks. (*USAMHI*)

(*Opposite page*) Marauders with full packs march along a jungle track during Stilwell's attempted second envelopment near Inkangahtawng in the Mogaung Valley late March 1944. (*USAMHI*)

(*Left*) A heavy machine-gun crew supports its 3rd Battalion riflemen as they attack Japanese positions leading to the besieged 2nd Marauder Battalion at Nhpum Ga. (*USAMHI*)

(*Above*) A 75mm Marauder pack howitzer crew fires directly at Japanese positions 400 yards away near Nhpum Ga. This sudden close-in employment of artillery demoralized the Japanese. (*USAMHI*)

(*Opposite page*) Marauder 81mm mortar crew awaits a fire mission request from 3rd Battalion's Orange Combat Team during its relief of the 2nd Battalion at Nhpum Ga April 1944. (*Nat. Arch. 111-SC-277384*)

(*Below*) A C-47 drops food and supplies to the HQ Company of the 1st Battalion near Hsamshingyang in late March 1944. (*Nat. Arch. 111-SC-277378*)

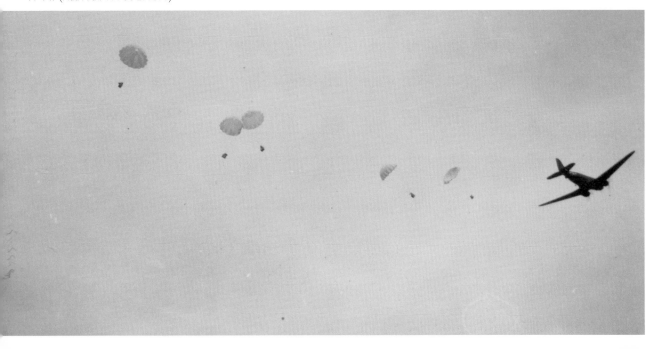

(*Above*) Marauders quickly collect supplies in an open field that were airdropped during the siege of Nhpum Ga. An officer uses a radio to contact the units waiting to be resupplied. (*USAMHI*)

(*Opposite page*) A C-47 flying low parachutes supplies to the besieged 2nd Marauder Battalion at Nhpum Ga. Water resupply was a problem as thirst plagued the surrounded Marauders. (*USAMHI*)

(*Left*) After an airdrop, 3rd Battalion's Khaki Combat Team members carry off supplies after the siege of Nhpum Ga had been broken in early April 1944. (*Nat. Arch. 111-SC-277392*)

(*Above*) To boost morale after the Nhpum Ga siege, Major Briggs conducts a full inspection of his surviving 3rd Battalion Khaki Combat Team troops before their trek to Myitkyina. (*Nat. Arch. 111-SC-277391*)

(*Opposite page*) After Nhpum Ga, a 3rd Battalion Khaki Combat Team sergeant cleans his 60mm mortar, which with the 81mm mortar, were heavily relied on due to limited artillery. (*Nat. Arch. 111-SC-277390*)

(*Left*) A Marauder inspects the P-17 Enfield rifle of his Chinese 38th Division comrade while he shows him his M1 Garand rifle after the fighting at Nhpum Ga in April 1944. (*Nat. Arch. 111-SC-277395*)

15790

(*Above*) Marauders unload the precious supply cargo from a C-47 transport that crashed but remained largely intact without fire damage after the siege of Nhpum was lifted. (*Nat. Arch. 111-SC-263273*)

(*Opposite page*) After their gruelling combat operations in the Hukawng and Mogaung Valley envelopments, a group of Marauders rest and eat rations after making a fire in the jungle. (*USAMHI*)

Chapter Eight

The Chindits, Airborne Invasion, *Operation Thursday* and Mogaung

On 4 August 1943 Wingate was taken by Churchill to Quebec for the Quadrant Conference to present his opinions about an enlarged LRP expedition for Burma in early 1944, as part of a multi-pronged Allied offensive in southern Asia, to the Combined Chiefs-of-Staff (CCS) and to President Roosevelt. Thanks to Roosevelt and his subordinates' interest, namely Generals Marshall and Arnold (head of the US Army Air Force), the US Army was to train their own LRP (later designated as the 5307th Composite Unit or *GALAHAD*) under Wingate as well as form an Air Commando from USAAF cadres to provide the Chindits with an expanded aerial dimension to their tactical doctrine. On his return to India, Wingate was promoted to major general in command of Special Force, the new title for the Chindits. In the Order of Battle, this Chindit organization would have as its cover name 3rd Indian Division, though it included few Indian troops. His old friend and colleague, Derek Tulloch, was to become the force's brigadier general staff.

Wingate was to get six brigades largely from the re-organization of the British 70th and a brigade from the 81st West African divisions. The 70th British Division was a veteran formation with long Middle East experience. Brigadier Calvert commanded 77th Brigade (composed of elements of the King's Regiment, the Lancashire Fusiliers, the South Staffords and the 6th and 9th Gurkha Rifles). Brigadier William Lentaigne led the 111th Brigade with the King's Own Royal Regiment and a battalion of Cameronians as its core. Brigadier Bernard Fergusson commanded the 16th Brigade, which was composed of elements of the Queen's Royal Regiment, 2nd Bn Leicestershire Regiment, elements of the Royal Artillery and the Royal Armoured Corps. The 14th and 23rd brigades were made up of men from the former British 70th Division. The sixth and final brigade was the 3rd West African Brigade, which arrived in India in November 1943. The Special Force numbered approximately 23,000 men.

Wingate anticipated that by concentrating three of his brigades around Indaw he might force the Japanese to evacuate Northern Burma. He hoped to threaten

Japanese LOC south of Wuntho and menace the Japanese 15th Army's resupply, thereby enabling Slim's 4 Corps to better withstand the suspected upcoming Japanese offensive thrust (*Operation U-Go*) into Assam. As early as 16 January 1944, Wingate provided evidence to Mountbatten that a Japanese move up to the Chindwin River was the preparatory stage for an offensive against Assam. He believed that the Japanese would be compelled to use the 'long bad vulnerable roads of Burma', that this offensive would be 'strong and damaging' and that before it was overcome British 11th Army Group might have to face the temporary loss of all Manipur. Wingate's predictions were quite accurate as later events showed. On 14–15 March the Japanese invaded Assam in three-division strength from the north of Homalin and from the centre of their Chindwin front, in *Operation U-Go*.

Air power would revolutionize LRP as fighter-bombers (P-47 Thunderbolts, P-51 Mustangs, and RAF Spitfires and Vengences) and medium bombers (B-25 Mitchells) became aerial artillery for close infantry support. The transports (C-46 *Commando* and C-47 *Dakota*), 100 L5 liaison aircraft, and over 200 Waco gliders would provide supplies, armaments, reinforcements and casualty evacuation with precision, enabled by state-of-the-art radio communications. The need for sea- or land-borne LOC for an invading force was over. His new USAAF allies were Colonels Philip Cochran and John Alison. In a meeting with Wingate, Cochran assured Wingate that the Chindits had only to 'dream up' ideas and he would put them into operation.

Unlike *Operation Longcloth*, Wingate envisioned Special Force being able to stay and fight at locales of choice (i.e. Wingate's strongholds) rather than dispersing or having to fight one's way back through an enclosing enemy. The new aspect to Wingate's LRP doctrine was to establish defended areas wherever his brigades were operating. The notion was that such a defended locale would enable columns to retire for safety and then set out on raids from its perimeter. With supply and relief these strongholds could become virtual offensives on their own. Their entry into Burma would be made by aircraft and gliders. A Chindit group of roughly two columns (approximately 800 men) would occupy a field that would be converted into a landing strip for larger transport aircraft. Then the rest of the brigade would be brought in by the transport aircraft. Wingate envisioned that these defended areas would be operational within thirty-six hours and ready to disrupt the IJA installations and LOC in the vicinity. Slim also offered to furnish the Chindit garrisons with a number of 25-pounder field and Bofors 40mm AA guns for defence against enemy infantry, artillery, and air attack.

In January 1944 Wingate formulated his plan with 77th Brigade to fly into the Kaukkwe Valley north-east of Katha to establish a stronghold and disrupt the railway from Indaw to Myitkyina as well as block the Bhamo-Lashio road. Lentaigne's 111th Brigade would also fly in to the area south of Pinlebu and form a stronghold to attack IJA LOC around Wuntho and also in the Mu Valley. Fergusson's 16th Brigade, which was the first to depart by overland march from Ledo on 5 February, would head south to establish a stronghold north of Indaw to attack the Bonchaung Gorge, the Meza Bridge and, ultimately, capture the Indaw airfield. Two smaller forces ('Morrisforce' and 'Dahforce' under Lt Colonels J.R. Morris and D.C. Herring respectively) would operate on IJA LOC along the Bhamo-Myitkyina road and in the Kachin Hill country to the east. The second wave of the Chindit force would be the 14th and 23rd Brigades and, along with the 3rd West African Brigade for garrison duty, would be held in reserve for relief or exploitation.

The airfields for the departures of 77th and 111th brigades were Hailakandi and Lalaghat. Air landing zones in the Kaukkwe valley were called 'Broadway' to the north and 'Piccadilly', about 35 miles south of the former. Glider-borne infantry would leave Lalaghat along with US Army engineers with Jeeps, bulldozers and graders to create the Dakota transport airfields for subsequent material and personnel reinforcement. An additional two air landing zones were 'Chowringhee', between the Irrawaddy and Schweli rivers, for 'Morrisforce', and 'Templecombe', for 'Dahforce', about 35 miles due south of Myitkyina.

On 5 March Calvert's 77th Brigade was to take-off by towed gliders from Lalaghat. In the late afternoon, one of Cochran's aerial reconnaissance planes obtained photographs of the Kaukkwe valley. Wingate had forbidden such flights over the operational area, but Cochran had nonetheless arranged it. In the photographs, all of Piccadilly's level space was covered by teak logs. Wingate, Calvert, Tulloch, Scott, Cochran, Alison and Air Marshal Baldwin all knew that glider landings there were now impossible and the entourage wondered if security for the operation had been breached. Over a span of twenty minutes, Wingate conferred with Slim and then left the decision to continue the operation to Calvert, who enthusiastically agreed to still go. With an abundance of panache Cochran redirected his pilots to 'a better place to go' and after a delay of just over an hour, sixty-one of an originally planned eighty gliders were towed by the Dakotas. By 11 March the fly-ins were complete and over 9,200 Chindits began to organize themselves with their own airstrips for fighter cover and resupply and to receive their 25-pdr field guns and 40mm Bofors AAA guns.

After supervising the construction of Broadway into a stronghold, Calvert led out five Chindit columns to the west of the railway to create a smaller stronghold to serve as a LOC block from the south to Myitkyina, which he took by bayonet charge and fierce hand-to-hand combat at the railway town of Henu, a mile or so to the north of the Mawlu rail station. This stronghold was eventually called 'White City' because of all the parachutes festooning the trees. Troop and supply movement by the IJA on the railway from Katha and Indaw to Myitkyina was held up with the construction of this White City.

The airborne landings and establishment of strongholds created panic among the 18th IJA Division's LOC as quartermaster troops from Japanese 15th Army headquarters had previously, on 10 January 1944, suspended movements of supplies to Tanaka in order to accumulate stocks for the attack on Imphal. Shipments were to resume as soon as the Imphal operation was underway but the Chindits cut the railway just as the supplies were to have flowed to Tanaka's 18th Division again. This once fine division was going to survive on only what was available in Northern Burma since Tanaka's supply position was fundamentally compromised by the Chindit fighting along the railway from Bhamo to Myitkyina.

On 20 March, Wingate flew to a landing ground prepared by Fergusson's 16th Brigade at Taungle in the Meza valley, where the stronghold Aberdeen was situated, to discuss the assault on Indaw by 16th Brigade. Wingate developed a plan to fly-in 14th Brigade only, along with the garrison troops of 3rd West African Brigade, to Aberdeen immediately with initial landings occurring on 23 March coinciding with elements of 16th Brigade leaving the stronghold for the Indaw attack. On 24 March, after a meeting with Air Marshal Baldwin at Imphal, Wingate decided to use his Mitchell bomber again to visit Cochran's No. 1 Air Commando at Lalaghat. Some-where between the Bishenpur Hills and Lalaghat, Wingate's aircraft crashed into a fiery wreckage in which everyone, including some USAAF officers and sergeants, were killed. It was Wingate's friend and Brigadier, Derek Tulloch, who declined taking over 3rd Indian Division and, instead, recommended Lentaigne of 111th Brigade.

Although 16th Brigade had initially failed in taking Indaw, a renewed assault suc-ceeded on 27 April. It turned out that the airfield at Indaw was only a fair weather one, so 16th Brigade was evacuated by air by the beginning of May and Aberdeen was abandoned. A few days later, Broadway and White City were also abandoned. These strongholds could not hold out during the monsoon rains because the airstrips could not be converted to all-weather fields.

After this, 77th, 14th and 111th brigades operated on Stilwell's Mogaung-Myitkyina front. Another stronghold called 'Blackpool' was established west of Mogaung, which was on the railway to Myitkyina. On 29 March, Stilwell's Chinese south-easterly moving divisions entered Shaduzup over the Jambu Bum Range in the Mogaung Valley. At the Mogaung Valley's south end on the Irrawaddy lay Myitkyina with its airfield, railway and roads. In order to capture the Mogaung-Myitkyina area, Stilwell had five Chinese divisions, the remaining troops of Merrill's Marauders and the three Chindit brigades at his disposal. To attest the élan and ruggedness of the Japanese 18th Division soldier, three under-strength and ill-supplied regiments, reinforced by two other regimental headquarters and three infantry battalions, would contest Stilwell's Allied force to their fullest.

Calvert's costly capture of Mogaung, which was the last major Chindit operation, was successfully completed on 27 June, a campaign in which these LRP guerrilla forces were mishandled by Stilwell as conventional infantry clearing a well-defended

Burmese city. Stilwell wanted Mogaung's capture during June 1944 to prevent the IJA troops there from reinforcing Myitkyina town or attacking the rear of the Sino-American position at the Myitkyina airfield. The close combat in June 1944 against the IJA would ultimately decimate 77th Brigade's ability to continue as a functional fighting unit after Mogaung was taken following a gruesome siege. On 16 June the Chinese evicted Tanaka from Kamaing into the hill country to the south and west. Also on that day the 114th Chinese Regiment linked up with 77th Brigade's troops at Gurkhaywa just north of both the Mogaung River and town. Over 1,000 of the 2,000 men of 77th Brigade who started the Battle of Mogaung on 31 May 1944 had become battle casualties in the four weeks of combat there. Another 150 seriously ill men also had to be evacuated leaving 77th Brigade's effective fighting strength at about 800 Chindit infantrymen.

Wingate *(left)* confers with USAAF Col Philip Cochran about the First Air Commando's role in expanding the Chindits' LRP capabilities of aerial artillery, troop and equipment resupply, and wounded evacuation. *(USAMHI)*

Col John Alison (*left*) and Col Philip Cochran (*right*), the First Air Commando leaders, with Wingate. This triumvirate revolutionized LRP operations with a myriad of aircraft and creative tactics.
(*Nat. Arch. RG-208-PU-223 N-1*)

Wingate (*centre*) addresses a contingent of Col Philip Cochran's (*behind Wingate's left shoulder*) USAAF No. I Commando about details of *Operation Thursday*. Capt Borror (Wingate's ADC, *far left*).
(*USAMHI*)

Wingate (*left*) and Cochran (*right*) brief British officers on air routes and landing fields at their Hailakandi, India air depot in late February 1944. (*Nat. Arch. RG-208-AA-11EE-S*)

Four Air Commando P-51 Mustangs fly in formation above a taxiing B-25 Mitchell bomber and an L5 Liaison plane at an Indian air depot before *Operation Thursday*. (*USAMHI*)

Close-up of P-51 Mustangs of the First Air Commando flying over the hills that separate Assam from Burma. These fighter-bombers would wreak havoc on Japanese troop concentrations. (*USAMHI*)

A P-47 Thunderbolt with a P-51 Mustang being serviced off the runway at an airfield in Assam. The P-47 was a rugged fighter-bomber capable of withstanding enemy ground fire. (*USAMHI*)

(*Above*) A Sentinel L5 Liaison plane, which was the workhorse of the Air Commando for evacuation of wounded from remote airstrips and Chindit strongholds. (*Nat. Arch. 111-SC-263250*)

(*Opposite page*) A C-47 Dakota practises towing a Waco glider. Unfortunately, some Wacos became detached from their tow planes during the initial flights to the landing zones for *Thursday*. (*USAMHI*)

(*Below*) C-47 Dakota practices towing a Waco glider. The versatile Waco could deliver infantry, supplies, animals, Jeeps and even artillery to the Chindit strongholds. (*USAMHI*)

(*Above*) Close-up view of a Waco landing. The craft's nose would lift outward and upward so ground personnel could easily and quickly unload. (*USAMHI*)

(*Opposite page*) Rows of teak logs blocking the air-landing field for gliders at Piccadilly on 5 March 1944 necessitating last minute modifications by Wingate and Cochran to start *Operation Thursday*. (*USAMHI*)

(*Below*) Chindits at Lalaghat airfield in India practice loading mules onto a Waco glider via its opened nose. A side door was present for troops to enter or exit the craft. (*USAMHI*)

Just before *Thursday's* start at Lalaghat, Wingate (*second from right*) reviews photographs from Piccadilly showing teak logs blocking the landing zones with (*l-to-r*) Cochran, Alison, Scott, Baldwin, Calvert, and Tulloch.
(*Author's collection*)

Wingate (*right*) appears to be at odds with General Slim on the Lalaghat airfield after discussing the teak logs at Piccadilly. Ultimately Slim let Wingate devise a new plan.
(*USAMHI*)

US Army engineers and Chindits sit next to a crashed glider at Broadway before work to remove the wreckages and create a landing field for transports would get started. (*USAMHI*)

An American engineer uses a surviving small bulldozer from the initial glider landings to smooth the Broadway's landing field surface for upcoming transport and glider landings to reinforce the stronghold. (*USAMHI*)

(*Above*) Chindits smooth furrows manually with shovels on Broadway's landing field on 6 March 1944. A bulldozer with an attached scraper works in the background. (*Nat. Arch. C-993134*)

(*Opposite page*) Chindit on a stretcher receives plasma at 'Broadway' on 6 March 1944. He was one of the thirty men who died or thirty-three injured in the previous night's glider crashes.
(*Nat. Arch. RG-208-AA-221-50653-AC*)

(*Left*) Two Chindits stand at the burned-out wreck of a Waco glider at Broadway. Many such scenes dotted the Broadway landing field after Calvert's initial glider landings on 5 March 1944. (*USAMHI*)

A wounded Chindit sits atop a makeshift stretcher and awaits air evacuation from 'Broadway', which clearly differentiated *Operation Thursday* from *Operation Longcloth*. *(USAMHI)*

An L5 Sentinel pilot poses with Chindits prior to evacuation of wounded. These pilots flew endless sorties to get the wounded to rear echelon hospitals.
(USAMHI)

Wingate stares into space holding his trademark rifle as he flies aboard his B-25 Mitchell bomber, which took him from stronghold to stronghold.
(Nat. Arch. RG 208-AA-N-24832-FA)

Wingate (*left*) is met by Calvert as he deplanes from a transport at a stronghold airfield. The Chindit leader perished in a fiery wreck of his B-25 Mitchell bomber in Assam on 24 March 1944. (*USAMHI*)

Wingate (*centre*) poses at Broadway with (*l-to-r*), Cols Alison and Calvert, Capt Borror (Wingate's ADC), Col Scott and Maj Francis as they await a night supply drop. (*Author's collection*)

Wingate instructs his Chindit officers on tactics at one of his 'strongholds'. The stronghold concept of *Operation Thursday* negated *Operation Longcloth's* 'dispersal and rendezvous' tactic. *(USAMHI)*

A Chindit Bofors gun crew watches supplies descend for the 'stronghold' on the railway at Henu. It was called White City because of the many white parachutes festooning the trees. (USAMHI)

Three crewmen of a 25-pounder field artillery gun dig a defensive pit that would be strengthened with sandbags. These guns gave the Chindit strongholds incredible defensive firepower. (USAMHI)

Chindits firing a 6-inch mortar round. These versatile weapons were used inside and outside of the strongholds and were very useful at breaking up enemy troop concentrations attacking Chindit positions. *(USAMHI)*

Three Chindit officers confer with an Air Commando officer about evacuation of wounded from a stronghold airfield with L5 Sentinel liaison aircraft. *(USAMHI)*

L5 Sentinel liaison aircraft taxi onto the White City airfield in one of their innumerable sorties to evacuate wounded Chindits to rear echelon hospitals. *(Nat. Arch. RG-208-AA-11B-14)*

Col Philip Cochran of the First Air Commando reviews plans to evacuate wounded Chindits from Aberdeen with two of their officers. *(USAMHI)*

In a jungle clearing, Chindits tend to their wounded with first aid and dressings while awaiting L5 Sentinel air evacuation. (*USAMHI*)

Chindits, Burmese villagers, Air Commando crew and mechanics pose after repairing a damaged C-47 in the field. The kneeling Chindits maintained a guard while the airmen did the repairs. (*Nat. Arch. RG-208-AA-11F-3*)

(*Above*) Two Chindits sit atop their wood- and sandbag-reinforced slit trench at a stronghold during *Operation Thursday*. Defensive fortifications were paramount with the numerous Japanese assaults on the strongholds. (*USAMHI*)

(*Opposite above*) During a lull in the fighting, Chindits are at ease at one of their jungle bases. The strongholds gave the Chindits tremendous mobility to establish ancillary sites and ambushes. (*USAMHI*)

(*Opposite below*) Chindits from the 3rd West African Bde on the north-eastward march to support Stilwell after Wingate's death as their strongholds became untenable without all-weather airfields. (*USAMHI*)

A demolition party of Lancashire Fusiliers prepare charges to destroy a Japanese HQ building at Mawhun. Fighting an entrenched enemy with light weaponry caused tremendous casualties in Calvert's 77th Bde. (*USAMHI*)

A dead Japanese soldier at Mogaung lies next to his Rising Sun battle flag. Japanese resistance in Mogaung's buildings was tenacious. (*USAMHI*)

To bring direct fire onto entrenched Japanese positions in Mogaung, a 3-inch mortar crew adjusts the weapon's elevation while another Chindit (*background*) is serving as a spotter. (*USAMHI*)

Brig Calvert (*left*) gives instructions to Majors Shaw (*centre*) and Lumley (*right*) at Mogaung's fall. Officers carried rifles over side-arms to avoid being targeted by enemy snipers. (*Author's collection*)

Chindit searches for weapons hidden in dishevelled uniforms of some Japanese prisoners captured after close quarter, house-to-house fighting in Mogaung, June 1944. (*USAMHI*)

Chindits inspect a Japanese corpse in Mogaung's ruins after its costly capture. The assault on Mogaung was not in keeping with the highly specialized LRP training that the Chindits possessed. (*USAMHI*)

Chindits return to an Assam airfield and speak with their Air Commando crews. Evacuation via C-47 was a far cry from the ambulatory one at *Operation Longcloth's* end. (*USAMHI*)

Chapter Nine

On To Myitkyina

For the third time the Marauders were to take part in a wide-flanking move or 'hook' to the east over the Kumon Range, which formed the eastern boundary of the Mogaung valley, with two attached Chinese regiments and a screen of Kachin tribesmen. The plan was called End Run, using Stilwell's characteristic American football parlance. This was to be the most difficult of the Marauders' missions; they were to strike at Myitkyina itself, the chief objective of the campaign. However, it has been said that Stilwell was fully cognizant of the drain placed on the Marauders with their ceaseless combat. Although Stilwell was aware of this, he was consumed by his own 'driving passion to reach Myitkyina'. Stilwell was an ardent believer that possession of Myitkyina would force the Japanese to leave Northern Burma enabling him to re-open both the Ledo and old Burma Roads.

Regarding the Marauders, the fighting edge of the most mobile and most obedient force that Stilwell had was now dulled. This force had subsisted on cold K-rations while trekking and fighting over 250 miles of jungle, often contracting malaria and dysentery while succumbing to the almost universally lethal scrub typhus. Despite these hardships, Stilwell intended to keep the Marauders in the field past its promised ninety-day limit, set by their initial organizer Wingate, for his final thrust to Myitkyina, 287 miles to the south-east of the Ledo Road's origin in Assam. Stilwell was counting on the capture of the all-weather Myitkyina airfield, which would greatly facilitate resupply and evacuation of the wounded as well as hasten the success of this campaign. Additional Chinese and Kachin troops brought Merrill's strength to about 7,000 men for the Myitkyina operation. Colonel Charles Hunter, Merrill's deputy, put his staff to work, planning a move to Myitkyina, and deployed Kachin scouts over the Kumon Range to find a concealed route to attack the Japanese hub on the Irrawaddy, 65 miles to the south-east. Stilwell also planned to simultaneously continue his drive down the Mogaung corridor toward Kamaing, with the Chinese 65th Regiment protecting the right flank of the Chinese 22nd Division as before. Stilwell wanted to deceive Tanaka that Kamaing was the main Sino-American objective, when his major plan was to capture Myitkyina all the time.

Critics have argued that Stilwell took a desperate gamble on the Myitkyina assault, and it almost resulted in disaster. A careful study might reveal that it was a tactical mistake. It was argued that both time and excessive casualties would have been saved had Stilwell kept his forces, fire-power and air-power concentrated to first capture Kamaing, then continue to take Mogaung, some 20 miles south, and then up the railway, with all his power, to capture Myitkyina. To take Kamaing, Stilwell had a much greater advantage over the Japanese, especially in artillery and air-power than he had at Myitkyina.

The assault on Myitkyina started as an arduous southerly trek across the Kumon Range, some points higher than 6,000-feet, with the Kachin scouts leading 1,400 of the original 2,997 Marauders divided into three combat teams and stiffened with Chinese troops. It was understood by the three Marauder battalion commanders that the capture of the Myitkyina airfield was the end of the campaign and they would be evacuated to India. The three combat teams were as follows: H Force under Colonel Hunter; K Force under Colonel Kinnison; and M Force under Colonel McGee. K Force left for the Kumon Range on 28 April followed by H Force, which departed on 30 April. Stilwell's plan called for H and K forces crossing the Kumon Range via the 6,100-foot Naura Hkyet Pass and then heading due south onto Ritpong. From there the two forces would take separate routes that would later converge on Myitkyina. M Force would be in position to cover the southern flank, which was regarded to be the most hazardous point. M Force started its trek on 7 May. On 5 May, Kinnison enveloped Ritpong and it took until 9 May for Ritpong's Japanese defenders to fall. In the meantime, H Force overtook and passed through K Force on its southward march to Myitkyina. On 12–13 May, as K Force feigned an attack on Nsopzup on the Irrawaddy well north of Myitkyina, they clashed with the Japanese at Tingkrukawng. Unable to overtake the Japanese, Kinnison was ordered by Merrill to disengage and pick up Colonel Hunter's trail and follow it to Myitkyina. Unfortunately, Kinnison contracted scrub typhus and died during his evacuation.

On the night of 15 May it appeared that total surprise was achieved as it was estimated that there were only 100 Japanese troops at the airfield. On 17 May, Hunter sent in the Chinese 150th Regiment of the 50th Division, which captured the Myitkyina airstrip. The Marauder component of H Force took the ferry terminal on the Irrawaddy at Pamati and another village, Zigyun, also on the river. The second airstrip north of the town of Myitkyina was not attacked on that day. Most regrettably the town of Myitkyina was not assaulted on 17 May, thereby allowing the Japanese to reinforce it. Unfortunately, Hunter, after capturing the western airfield at Myitkyina, had only a fraction of the Marauders that began the trek over the Kumon Range. Stilwell's diary entry for this day read 'WILL THIS BURN UP THE LIMIES'.

After a remarkable twenty-day march, the force of Marauders, Chinese and OSS-led Kachins of Detachment 101 appeared on the airstrip on 17 May. The Japanese were completely surprised and before they could react the Marauders had established themselves several miles south of the town. As fighting was going around the perimeter, American transport planes and gliders brought in Chinese reinforcements and 17 May was a significant date in the Northern Burma campaign as battles for Kamaing, Mogaung and Myitkyina were all to be contested simultaneously, which would ultimately clear all of Northern Burma of the Japanese.

However, the town of Myitkyina was still, and would remain, in Japanese hands until the beginning of August due to a variety of logistical problems at all levels of command. On 18 May Merrill returned to duty and reorganized the units at Myitkyina airfield as Hunter remained the Marauders' ground force commander. However, after another heart attack Merrill was evacuated the next day. In the town of Myitkyina, Colonel Maruyama, the local Japanese commander, had two under-strength battalions of the 114th Regiment of the 18th IJA Division along with other ancillary units. Erroneously, it was believed by Stilwell's G-2 that there were only a total of 700 IJA troops, a number that would be rigidly adhered to. However, the Japanese were reinforcing the town of Myitkyina more quickly than Stilwell's Chinese and Americans could attack. This was due, in large part, to the rain, which often closed the Myitkyina field to C-47 troop carrier planes. Also, Colonel Maruyama, using the Irrawaddy as a ferry service, much like the Russians used the Volga at Stalingrad, brought in major elements of the 56th Division from the Salween front into Myitkyina and General Mizukami assumed operational command in Myitkyina. Overall control of Japanese operations at Myitkyina was assumed by 33rd Army in early June, thereby freeing Tanaka to concentrate on operations involving his 18th Division around Kamaing. A group of Chindits, Morris Force, was supposed to interdict Japanese movement to the western bank of the river. However, they were incapable of performing this challenging task. Ultimately, this enabled the Japanese to establish a battle that was more, in fact, like trench warfare than one of manoeuvre, the latter of which contributed greatly to Stilwell's success down the Hukawng and Mogaung Valleys. At peak time during the battle the Japanese forces totalled about 4,600 men, but American intelligence still clung to their much lower estimate defending Myitkyina town. Another explanation for the failure to take the town in a timely fashion was that Stilwell was obsessed with the airstrip and failed to plan a subsequent attack on the town.

The mishandled process of reinforcement of the Myitkyina airfield by Stilwell was not entirely his fault. Rather than sending in strong infantry reinforcements and supplies, General Stratemeyer, commanding the Army Air Forces, India-Burma Sector initially deployed only a company of Engineers (the 879th Airborne Engineer Aviation Battalion) that arrived via glider. Tenth Air Force had at once given over elements of this battalion to repair and hold the precious airfield, the only means of contact between Merrill's force and the rear echelons back in the Hukawng or Assam. Later that day saw the arrival of the 2nd Battalion of the Chinese 89th Regiment along with some machine-gun units for anti-aircraft purposes. Then, bad weather intervened for the remainder of the 17th.

On 18 May Stratemeyer ordered the British 69th Light (Anti-Aircraft) Regiment to be flown in. Merrill and Hunter wanted infantry and supplies to pursue a rapid assault on the town, but back at headquarters in India the intent was to defend the airfield from attack since its condition on capture was quite good. An attempt to seize Myitkyina was made by two battalions of the Chinese 150th Regiment on the afternoon of 17 May. However, these relatively raw troops lost their way and ended up firing on themselves, inflicting disastrous casualties in the process.

Hunter did mobilize his remaining troops from K and M Forces and these elements, rather than waiting for aerial resupply, set out for the town of Myitkyina. In Hunter's memoirs he noted that after Stilwell visited the airfield he ordered him to attack the town of Myitkyina. Hunter expressed his misgivings at beginning an attack with little chance of success while being compelled to use only Chinese troops with the evident problem of needing to use an interpreter to convey orders and make sure they were understood. The attack launched on the morning of 18 May had some success. It penetrated all the way to Sitapur on the edge of Myitkyina itself, but after an immediate all-round counterattack by the highly mobile Japanese floating reserve, Hunter's small assault force dug in to form a small defensive perimeter. On 18 May the remainder of the 89th Regiment and a company of heavy mortars were flown in followed by the 3/42nd of the Chinese 14th Division the next day.

Controversy exists as to why the excellent British 36th Division was not used to take Myitkyina town, only instead to be sent south by Stilwell in July 1944 on the 'Railway Corridor' between Myitkyina and Katha. Early in July, the 72nd Brigade led the 36th Division onto Myitkyina airfield. The 36th Division was the first all-British unit to come under the command of General Joseph Stilwell. Its task was to clear the Railway Corridor extending from Myitkyina south for approximately 145 miles. Stilwell briefly considered asking that the British 36th Division be rushed in to take Myitkyina even though this division had been withdrawn from Arakan to re-fit before being allocated to Stilwell's NCAC. Ultimately, these British veterans were fit and ready for battle and were the obvious force with which to replace Hunter's exhausted men. Giving no reason in his diary, he decided against utilizing the British 36th Division and instead ordered in some US combat engineers from the Ledo Road. Perhaps, the Anglophobic Stilwell did not want to be beholden to British troops to restore some élan to his waning attack on Myitkyina town with his Sino-American forces. Stilwell's failure to take the town of Myitkyina after his initial sensational success at capturing the western airfield was to be one of his greatest humiliations.

Stilwell ordered two battalions of American combat engineers; the 504th Engineer Light Pontoon Company flew in from Ledo to set up operations on the Irrawaddy, south of the airfield at Pamati along with the 209th Engineers who arrived on transports bound for Myitkyina airfield. Though these engineers were supposed to have had combat training they proved to be very inexperienced and ill-suited as frontline infantry. Two days later, the 236th Engineers, General Lewis Pick's sole remaining combat engineers on the Ledo Road, were taken away for infantry service in the mounting struggle. Initially because the Engineers were rushed to Myitkyina without extensive training, they were very tentative in engaging the entrenched Japanese often not following orders or refusing to mount assaults when under heavy enemy fire. However, by late July, when the Japanese defence of Myitkyina was slackening, the 209th and 236th were ordered to move back to the airfield for evacuation. All the engineer companies won Presidential Unit Citations in this engagement but at the price of 272 Americans killed and 955 wounded in the summer-long siege. Almost half of the dead engineers and over a third of the wounded were from the 209th and 236th Engineers. These rear area combat engineers, hastily ordered to Myitkyina, were no replacement for the veteran Marauder battalions. However, after getting 'blooded', the 209th and 236th Combat Engineers fought with greater élan. These two units would sustain casualty rates as heavy as any other American unit anywhere throughout the global conflict.

More Chinese infantrymen were thrown into the attack also, but the Japanese, stronger than Stilwell's G-2 estimates had surmised, had settled into deep bunkers and redoubts along a strong perimeter. However, with only a dozen P-40s now at Myitkyina, along with a paucity of artillery pieces and no tanks, it would be almost near impossible to break into the Japanese entrenchments, especially with the continuation of steady rainfall. Also, the Japanese were not merely static, but made repeated attacks on the Allied positions in late May. The latter third of May developed into a see-saw conflict of ad hoc Sino-American units under the overall command of Colonel John E. McCammon with Hunter as executive officer. Due to repeated assault failures, McCammon was replaced on 30 May with General Ted Wessels.

June also deteriorated into a month of frustration as the monsoon interfered with resupply operations. Attacks by Chinese regiments were made on the town only to be pushed back by the Japanese after heavy casualties. American intelligence officers began sensing that the Japanese garrison was stronger than expected, but clung to the wildly low estimate that only 1,000 Japanese combat troops faced them. On 17 June the Marauders' 3rd Battalion reached the Irrawaddy River north of Myitkyina coinciding with further gains by the Chinese 150th Regiment. Also, at this time, the Americans captured the Myitkyina-Mogaung-Sumprabum road junction. However, because of increasing manpower losses among the Americans and Chinese, Stilwell ordered a halt to his infantry attacks and resorted to tunnelling, which would be used to get at the enemy utilizing a classic siege warfare tactic. The Chinese troops had even attempted mining operations. The siege operations were monotonous with every day representing an attempt to move the front forward with daily progress measured in yards. Also, food and supplies during June were down to a minimum because Japanese mortars interrupted the flights of the transports to Myitkyina airfield. At times no more than a day's rations were on hand. Early in June it even appeared that the Japanese might recapture the vital Myitkyina airfield.

Throughout June a battle of attrition from both combat and disease continued to exhaust both sides. By the very end of the month Chinese troops in the Mogaung Valley were now able to move up the railroad to join Myitkyina's beleaguered attackers, thereby removing the recurrent menace of a Japanese drive from Mogaung while also opening a ground line of communications. Wessels' men, instead of fearing an enemy assault on their rear from Mogaung, could now concentrate their attention on the Japanese to their front. General Wessels launched a major attack on 12 July with air support. However, it failed, necessitating a return to the slow slugfest, which drove the Japanese back on daily basis.

The initial signs that the IJA was beginning to lose the battle for the town of Myitkyina occurred during the last week of July when Japanese wounded were floated down the Irrawaddy via raft and key IJA officers were committing ritual suicide. When the Marauder's 3rd Battalion captured the northern airfield at Myitkyina on 26 July, Japanese resistance was noticeably weaker. On 1 August Stilwell was promoted to four-star general. Also on that day General Mizukami committed suicide after he made sure that the main part of his defenders, under Colonel Maruyama, could be safely withdrawn from the area. On 3 August Myitkyina was finally captured, after General Wessels had ordered a fresh attack on the town for that day. The Japanese had left a small rear-guard of less than 200 sick men. Colonel Maruyama was able to withdraw 600 men. The Americans suffered a total of 2,207 casualties while their Chinese comrades lost 4,344. The Japanese suffered 790 killed, 1,180 wounded and 187 captured.

Hunter concluded that to capture the city rather than the airstrip should have been his mission since the early Allied occupation of Myitkyina town would have discouraged all the remaining Japanese in north-east Burma from using it as a rallying point, which continually increased the enemy garrison's strength. For the Japanese the airfield would have been untenable with the town in Allied hands from the start as it was not a natural terrain feature that facilitated either temporary defence or continuing offensive action. Myitkyina town on the banks of the Irrawaddy, as the campaign more than adequately demonstrated, was defensible without control of the airfield.

The Sino-American artillery at Myitkyina was also very weak. There were only a handful of 75mm, 105mm and 155mm guns. Some 4.2 inch mortars were also part of the heavy weaponry. There was less than a battalion of artillery for such a major operation as the capture of Myitkyina town. One of the reasons for the shortage of artillery was the lack of transport because of the monsoon and bad airstrip conditions, which took an increasing toll on the number of transport planes available for resupply.

Accounts of planes sliding into mud pits up to their propellers were not uncommon. Furthermore, combat air support was diminished because of wide-ranging commitments elsewhere.

However, Stilwell did enjoy the praise of many. Churchill questioned Mountbatten during the height of *Operation U-Go* at Imphal, as to how 'the Americans by a brilliant feat of arms have landed us in Myitkyina'.

Mountbatten, in turn, in his communiqué to Stilwell and his troops declared it 'a feat which will live in military history'.

Slim complimented his American counterpart. 'The capture of Myitkyina, so long delayed, marked the complete success of the first stage of Stilwell's campaign. It was also the largest seizure of enemy-held territory that had yet occurred ... When all is said and done, the success of this northern offensive was in the main, due to the Ledo Chinese divisions ... and that was Stilwell.'

Stilwell (*left*) with Col Hunter (*centre*), the Myitkyina airfield's attack planner and Merrill's (*right*) deputy, on the airstrip 18 May 1944. Hunter wanted to capture the town before the airfield. (*USAMHI*)

Hunter (*right*), Lt Col Combs (*left*), and Major Hodges planning the airfield's attack. Combs, a liaison officer with the Chinese, died warning Combat Engineers of an ambush in mid-June. (*USAMHI*)

Gen Sun (*left*), 38th Division commander, with Merrill (*right*) and Col Henry Kinnison, K Force commander attacking the airfield. Kinnison contracted scrub typhus en route and died during evacuation. (*USAMHI*)

(*Left*) Brig Gen Ted Wessels (*left*), photographer Jack Belden (*centre*) and Col Hunter at Deogarh, India. Wessels was in command when Myitkyina fell on 3 August 1944. (*USAMHI*)

(*Opposite page*) Marauders await their first parachuted supplies in four days during their trek across the Kumon Range and then south to the Myitkyina airfield. (*USAMHI*)

(*Below*) Stilwell (*left*) and Hunter (*right*) confer with Chinese officers at the captured Myitkyina airfield. Hesitant and unsuccessful Allied attacks on Myitkyina town would necessitate a seventy-eight-day siege. (*Nat. Arch. 111-SC-429050*)

Stilwell (*centre*) confers with Hunter (*back to camera*) and Merrill (smoking his pipe) at Myitkyina airfield within days of its capture. Merrill would soon need evacuation for a heart attack. (*USAMHI*)

American airborne engineers fire their machine-guns at low-flying attacking Japanese aircraft bombing Myitkyina airfield during the second half of May 1944. An idle C-47 transport is in the background. (*USAMHI*)

With limited artillery at Myitkyina airfield, a Marauder mortar crew provides support for a Sino-American attack on Japanese entrenchments near Myitkyina town in late May 1944. *(USAMHI)*

A Marauder 75mm pack Howitzer provides some artillery support for the Americans and Chinese advancing on Myitkyina town. A pile of shell casings is in the foreground. *(Nat. Arch. 111-SC-274335)*

(*Above*) British Bofors gun crew scan Myitkyina airfield's runway (*background*) during an alert on 18 July 1944. An ox-drawn cart to carry wounded to transports near runway is close by. (*Nat. Arch. 111-SC-262536*)

(*Opposite above*) At the perimeter of the airfield, American troops fire an assortment of light and heavy machine-guns against Japanese planes intent on destroying arriving transports at the Myitkyina air terminus. (*USAMHI*)

(*Opposite below*) A crewman of a British 40mm Bofors AAA gun slips an ammunition clip into position while on red alert at Myitkyina airfield 18 July 1944. (*Nat. Arch. 111-SC-262534*)

(*Above*) American soldiers and reporters take cover from Japanese sniper fire by lying prone with personal weapons drawn under the fuselage of a transport plane. (*Nat. Arch. RG-208-AA-11P-9*)

(*Opposite above*) The Chinese crew of a camouflaged 105mm Howitzer fires at Japanese entrenchments at Myitkyina town. This was one of the few heavy ordnance pieces for the Sino-American force. (*Nat. Arch. 111-SC-192537*)

(*Opposite below*) A Signals soldier transmitting from his tent at Myitkyina airfield. Prior to Mogaung's fall at the end of June, Stilwell's Sino-American force was surrounded and dependent solely on air supply. (*USAMHI*)

Brought into the Seagrave Hospital area at the Myitkyina airfield, Marauder wounded are transported by oxcarts while a sentry looks on nearby. (*Nat. Arch. 111-SC-326013*)

Allied wounded brought by oxcarts from the hospital area to the edge of the runway to board a waiting C-47 transport to evacuate them to a rear echelon base hospital. (*Nat. Arch. RG-208-AA-12J-3*)

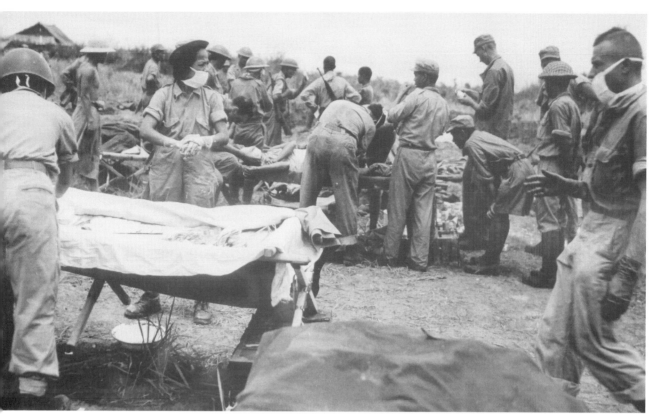

Open air operating tables characterized the expediency to render urgent surgical care at the Seagrave Hospital prior to evacuation for the sicker men. *(Nat. Arch. 208-AA-11GG-17)*

A medical team dresses wounds of an injured soldier while others wait on the ground next to the tall grass at the perimeter of the airfield. *(Nat. Arch. 208-AA-11GG-31)*

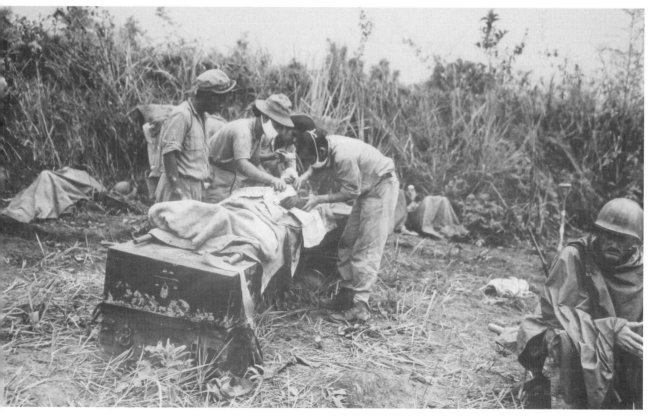

Several stretchers and makeshift operating tables are situated in close proximity to a C-47 not far from the airfield's runway. The Burmese nurses were from Colonel Seagrave's unit. (*USAMHI*)

A wounded American GI is about to be loaded onto a Sentinel L5 Liaison plane for evacuation from Northern Burma to a rear echelon hospital. (*Nat. Arch. RG-208-AA-12A-7*)

At Myitkyina airfield, a wounded Chinese soldier on stretcher is about to be loaded onto a Sentinel L5 Liaison plane for evacuation to a base hospital. (*Nat. Arch. 111-SC-277393*)

An ambulance brings a wounded Chinese soldier to a waiting Sentinel L5 liaison plane for urgent evacuation from the Myitkyina battle zone. *(Nat. Arch. RG-2-8-AA-11D-1)*

American soldiers lead a mule train with supplies brought onto the Myitkyina airfield by nearby transports. Ammunition, food and weapons were being brought to American infantry fighting for Myitkyina town. *(Nat. Arch. RG-208-AA-12B-3)*

Kachins and Chinese soldiers lift up the nose of a Waco glider to unload supplies and troops brought to the Myitkyina airfield on 21 June 1944. (*Nat. Arch. RG-208-AA-11E-2*)

American combat engineers unload equipment from a transport at the Myitkyina airfield as a siege was established for the town rather than costly direct assaults on Japanese fortifications. (*USAMHI*)

(*Above*) An American with his M1 Garand rifle scans the ruins of Myitkyina town for any hiding Japanese in the debris. (*USAMHI*)

(*Opposite above*) A Chinese soldier emerges from his siege dugout to fire his Thompson sub-machine-gun at Japanese soldiers near a pagoda in Myitkyina town. (*USAMHI*)

(*Opposite below*) American troops become the new occupants of a Japanese pillbox at Myitkyina. Note the Japanese helmet and rifle of the previous enemy occupant to the left. (*USAMHI*)

(*Above*) A Chinese soldier fires at Japanese troops holed up in boxcars at Myitkyina. All types of ruins and structures were used by the Japanese to prolong the siege. (*USAMHI*)

(*Opposite above*) A Marauder heavy machine gun crew provides direct fire on entrenched Japanese positions in the village of Sitapur, north-west of Myitkyina. (*USAMHI*)

(*Opposite below*) Stilwell discusses the tactical situation with American combat engineers that were hastily pressed into an infantry role to assault Myitkyina and wrest it from the Japanese 18 July 1944. (*Nat. Arch. 111-SC-262528*)

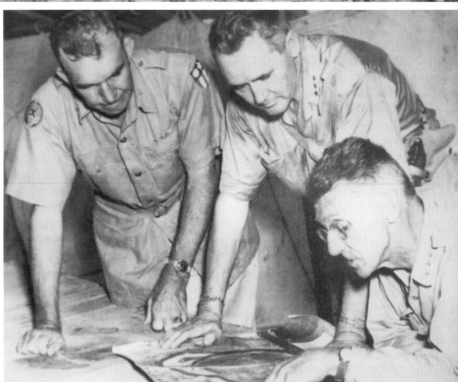

(*Above*) American and Chinese troops warily walk down a Myitkyina road past a ruined structure while another keeps a watchful eye from crouched position after the Japanese capitulation. (*USAMHI*)

(*Opposite above*) Stilwell reviews assault plans with American and Chinese officers at Sitapur on 18 July 1944. Despite a siege of two months, Myitkyina town would not capitulate until 3 August 1944. (*Nat. Arch. 111-SC-262527*)

(*Opposite below*) Stilwell (*right*) confers with Lt Gen Barney Giles (*left*), Chief of Airstaff, and Maj Gen Howard Davidson, Commander 10th Airforce at Myitkyina airstrip. Stilwell was recently promoted to general. (*Nat. Arch. 208-AA-11U-2*)

(*Above*) A truck with an improvised crane loads 250lb bombs onto P-47 Thunderbolt fighter-bombers at Myitkyina airfield to continue the offensive south to Bhamo and join the Burma Road. (*Nat. Arch. 111-SC-277216*)

(*Opposite above*) American and Chinese soldiers walk down a Myitkyina road in single-file past a ruined government building on the day of the Japanese surrender, 4 August 1944. (*Nat. Arch. Rg-208-AA-11SS-8*)

(*Opposite below*) An American soldier with M1 Garand rifle on knee takes a drink from his canteen in front of a destroyed business in Myitkyina town after the Japanese surrender. (*USAMHI*)

(*Above*) A C-47 transport takes off close to a massive bomb crater caused by a Japanese air attack on the airfield, 25 October 1944. (*Nat. Arch. 111-SC-263345*)

(*Opposite above*) A C-46 transport takes off from Myitkyina airfield with several parked P-40 Tomahawk fighters at the end of the runway. (*USAMHI*)

(*Opposite below*) Although close to capitulating, the Japanese attack the Myitkyina airfield with artillery on 1 August 1944 with a main runway targeted. (*USAMHI*)

(*Above*) A C-47 takes off from the Myitkyina airfield amid the smoking wrecks of aircraft destroyed there. The body of a Japanese soldier lies in the foreground at the runway's perimeter. (*Nat. Arch. 208-AA-11B-15*)

(*Opposite above*) A portion of the Myitkyina airfield complex with scattered empty fuel drums and parked fighters and transports under various states of repair, 12 Sept 1944. (*Nat. Arch. 111-SC-277417*)

(*Opposite below*) A line of C-47s taxiing past P-47 Thunderbolt fighter-bombers at the Myitkyina airfield, 12 Sept 1944 demonstrating the importance of capturing this complex. (*Nat. Arch. 111-SC-263299*)

(*Above*) Japanese corpses next to an improvised entrenchment of wood and corrugated tin. A wide array of defensive works forced Stilwell to create a siege rather than costly frontal assaults. (*USAMHI*)

(*Opposite above*) Myitkyina town devastation from aerial view two weeks after the capitulation by the Japanese garrison. The Irrawaddy River flows in the background. (*Nat. Arch. 111-SC-263386*)

(*Opposite below*) Myitkyina town carnage from the air. A temple remains standing not far from the Irrawaddy. Previous Japanese entrenchments are to the right. (*Nat. Arch. 111-SC-263387*)

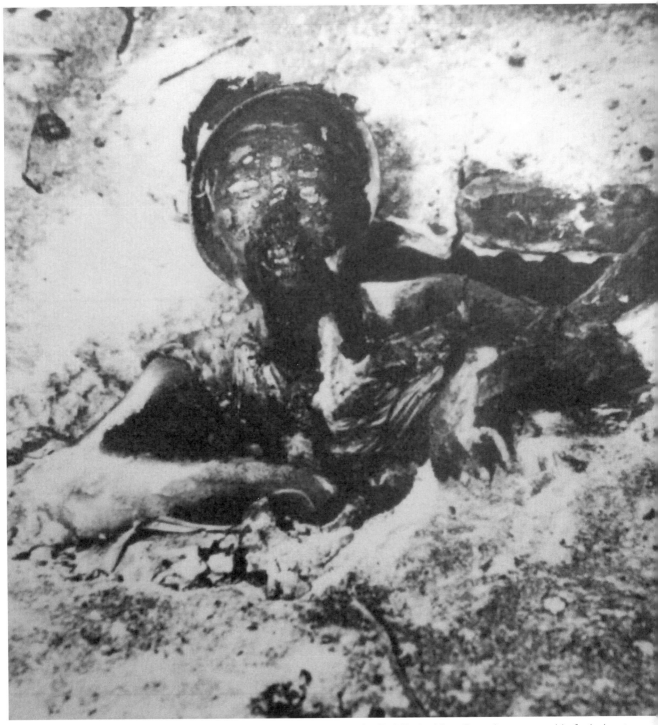

(*Above*) The charred remains of a Japanese trench defender finally killed with a flamethrower on his foxhole at Myitkyina. Fighting until extermination was commonplace at Myitkyina. (*USAMHI*)

(*Opposite page*) Japanese corpses in a mud-filled trench outside a ruined Myitkyina building are examined by a Kachin wielding his Thompson sub-machine-gun. (*USAMHI*)

Three Japanese who were captured trying to escape down the Irrawaddy on a raft. Their relatively intact uniforms and appearance suggest that they were recent reinforcements to the garrison. *(Nat. Arch. 111-SC-262538)*

Japanese prisoners captured on 3 August 1944 at Myitkyina. They appear emaciated with many of those who surrendered being wounded. (USAMHI)

An ingeniously-concealed Japanese foxhole at Myitkyina exhibits how the Sino-American advance from the airfield to town was measured daily in only yards. (USAMHI)

An American soldier comes across a Japanese soldier who preferred hanging himself than surrender in Myitkyina town. The adherence to *bushido* compelled officers and soldiers to commit suicide. *(USAMHI)*

A Japanese camouflaged and wood-reinforced mortar pit captured by the Allies and then converted to one of their own for the offensive on Myitkyina town. (*USAMHI*)

Chinese troops aboard the Mogaung-to-Myitkyina Jeep railway. After Mogaung's fall to the Chindits on 27 June 1944, reinforcements were able to reach Myitkyina overland rather than solely by air. (*Nat. Arch. 111-SC-277414*)

British 36th Division soldiers cross destroyed Japanese rolling stock at Mawlu six months after the Chindits had the White City stronghold there.
(*Nat. Arch. RG-208-AA-SE 265 RN*)

Seven months later, a 36th British Division soldier inspects the wrecked Jeep and debris from a crashed *Operation Thursday* Waco glider from 5 March 1944 in the Mu Valley.
(*Nat. Arch. 111-SC- 263324*)

Leading their mule train, British 36th Division's Royal Welsh Fusiliers cross Nankye Chaung on the way to Mawlu down the Railway Corridor in November 1944. (*Nat. Arch. RG-208-AA-221-SE262 RN*)

Troops of the British 36th Division march to Mawlu in November 1944 past one of their wounded being brought back on a stretcher. (*Nat. Arch. RG-208-AA-221-SE285 RN*)

(*Above*) An American soldier pays his last respects to those laid to rest in the shadow of a Burmese temple after being killed during the assault on Myitkyina in 1944. (*USAMHI*)

(*Opposite above*) Troops of the Royal Scots Fusiliers of the British 36th Division march down the Myitkyina-to-Mandalay Railway Corridor. Here they ford a jungle stream with the skirl of their bagpipes. (*Nat. Arch. BIZZ 848 LA*)

(*Opposite below*) Members of the British 36th Division move down the Railway Corridor by way of Jeeps specially fitted with railway wheels in the autumn of 1944. (*USAMHI*)

Epilogue

On 25 February 1944 President Roosevelt, in a memorandum to the British Prime Minister, made it clear, 'I have always advocated the development of China as a base for the support of our Pacific advances, and now that the war has taken a greater turn in our favour ... it is mandatory therefore that we make every effort to increase the flow of supplies into China. This can only be done by increasing the air tonnage or by opening a road through Burma. Our occupation of Myitkyina will enable us immediately to increase the air-lift to China by providing an intermediate air-transport base as well as by increasing the protection of the air route. General Stilwell is confident that his Chinese-American Force can seize Myitkyina by the end of this dry season.'

The American High Command, no doubt influenced by the political intervention of the 'China lobby', had as one of its missions the equipping and training, along American lines, of Chiang Kai-shek's ramshackle armies. Stilwell had already demonstrated at Ramgarh that he could improve the combat efficiency of the Chinese Army and, in so doing, had created the Chinese Army in India, a force of five divisions that fought and compared favourably with their Japanese foe. In order to train dozens of Chinese divisions on their own soil, the American mission called for the Ledo Road and pipeline from India to China and the seizure of Myitkyina to be prerequisites to deliver adequate supplies and fuel to Chiang Kai-shek's Nationalist forces there. Stilwell's task was accomplished despite many of his contemporaries thinking it was an impossible one. Also, the taking of Myitkyina on 3 August 1944 successfully evicted the Japanese Army from Northern Burma and made possible an intensified air effort from bases in China in support of US operations in the Pacific. After Myitkyina's capitulation, the Allied offensive in Northern Burma had recouped territory within 40 miles of the Chinese border. The Allies had reclaimed a portion of the Burmese road network, which linked with the old Burma Road. Ultimately, further Allied advances down the Railway Corridor and with a Chinese offensive from Yunnan would eventually drive out the last Japanese and the existing road from Myitkyina, now connected to Assam via the Ledo Road, could be re-established to effectively end the Japanese land blockade of China.

Stilwell was a troop trainer and a tactician, not an engineer. The construction of the Ledo Road, although under Stilwell's overall command, was conducted as engineering and supply marvels by Brigadier General Lewis Pick and Major General Raymond Wheeler (Commanding General, Services of Supply, CBI) respectively. The Ledo

Road was nearly completed by 24 October 1944. The two great terrain problems, the Patkai Hills and the marshy lowlands of the Hukawng Valley, had been conquered. Trucks could now drive in eighteen hours from the Ledo base area to Warazup, which in turn was only 70 miles from Myitkyina. The simultaneous pipeline that was also constructed far outstripped the Ledo Road's truck route to deliver gasoline. On 2 October one of the two pipelines was in operation from the Indian refineries via Ledo to Myitkyina. Henceforth, Myitkyina would become a great supply centre fed by road, air and by pipeline. As a result of the Northern Burma campaign's efforts, the Allies would certainly be able to comply with Roosevelt and Marshall's directives to 'Support China' and keep them in the war. The Assam LOC, bringing up supplies for transport down the Ledo Road, which was soon to reach Myitkyina, along with the ATC 'Hump' route functioning at an all-time efficiency, by eliminating Japanese Army fighter interdiction, would break the blockade of China.

On 12 January 1945 the first truck convoy from Ledo to China, 'Pick's First Convoy', started its 1,100-mile trek. It would be a two-week trip and would cross India's forested mountains before traversing the Hukawng Valley, replete with swamps and rivers. The Ledo Road would pass, at mile marker 109, Stilwell's first field HQ in Northern Burma at Shingbwiyang and then cross the Tarung and Tanai Rivers via newly-constructed pontoon and road bridges, in the vicinity of Walawbum, the site of the Marauders' first victory over Tanaka's Japanese infantry. The Ledo Road would trek south over the Jambu Bum mountains and into the Mogaung Valley past Inkangahtawng and Kamaing, where Tanaka had valiantly fought Stilwell's Sino-American force with three regiments of the once-invincible 18th IJA Division. As the Ledo Road passed Mogaung, it descended into the Irrawaddy Valley, Myitkyina or 'Stilwell's Quest' was only miles away. Myitkyina, although demonstrating the carnage of war with shattered buildings, railroad stock and streets, was 287 miles from Ledo, but now only three days of driving along 'Pick's Pike'. At Myitkyina, the overland route from Assam was still only 25 per cent of the way to Kunming. Due to continued Japanese resistance south of Myitkyina, the Ledo Road would not reach the old Burma Road at Mong Yu and enter the Chinese town of Wanting in Yunnan Province until 28 January 1945. At the Yunnan terminus, the road was renamed the Stilwell Road, by none other than Chiang Kai-shek. Some cynics would contend that the Ledo or Stilwell Road's overland supply route from India to China had become obsolete as, by the end of January 1945, the Allied CCS had instead decided to attack Japan from their home Pacific islands, the Ryukyu Islands, and not from the Chinese mainland or Formosa.

It is apparent that a number of histories clearly agree that Wingate's Chindit invasions of Burma in 1943 and 1944 did fulfil certain aspects of those missions' goals, even though a number of British senior commanders in Delhi, during and after the war, may have been derisive and willing to ignore the important outcomes of *Operation Longcloth* and *Thursday*. Japanese General Mutaguchi conceded after the war that *Operation Longcloth* had changed his entire strategic thinking. Mutaguchi had scrutinized Wingate's tactics and use of the Burmese terrain during the 1943 land-based invasion and concluded, as the Chindits had demonstrated, that troops would be mobile with pack transport in northern and western Burma only during the dry season. Wingate had also shown that it was possible for units to attack across the main north-south grain of the rivers and mountains of Burma. Because of *Operation Longcloth* in 1943, Mutaguchi argued that the 15th Japanese Army line of defence should be moved westward, to at least the Chindwin River, or even possibly to the hills on the Assam-Burma border. Having witnessed the Chindit invasion of 1943, the Japanese for their part had come to the conclusion that they would be unable to defeat the threatened future Allied offensive by remaining defensive-minded, and that an invasion of Assam in order to capture the Allied base at Imphal was their best course of action. The end of the summer of 1943 found the IJA planning an offensive for the dry season of early 1944 into eastern India.

The Japanese generals' reaction to *Operation Thursday* was discordant as their own *Operation U-Go* was underway. Mutaguchi initially believed that Wingate's second operation was too far into the northern Burmese interior to affect his own operations in Assam in the Kohima/Imphal area. However, his superior, General Kawabe of the Burma 33rd Army, took the second Chindit airborne invasion seriously and cobbled together a force of about 20,000 troops to confront Wingate at Indaw in March/April 1944. Initially, this force was able to prevent Fergusson's assault on Indaw, but it was then diverted to attack Calvert at White City. One has to wonder what would have transpired in Assam if these additional IJA troops, instead of combating Wingate's Chindits in Northern Burma, would have been made available to Mutaguchi's 15th Army fighting desperately at Imphal and Kohima. Also, after the war, Mutaguchi wrote to one of the official British historians about the *U-Go* offensive: 'Wingate's airborne tactics put a great obstacle in the way of our Imphal plan and were an important reason for its failure.'

Some of Wingate's critics have argued that the Chindits' *Operation Thursday* had its greater effect on the 18th IJA Division's LOC and that the 15th Army's drive on Imphal and Kohima was not affected by the Chindits' success with their strongholds. It is true that the greater effect of Wingate's second Burma mission was achieved by denying supplies and ammunition to be readied north to Tanaka's three regiments when made available by Mutaguchi and that this greatly assisted Stilwell's south-easterly Sino-American offensive. However, Japanese commanders after the war also commented that the Chindits' interdiction of 18th IJA Division's LOC did affect the subsequent withdrawal of 15th Army eastward after *U-Go*'s failure largely due to destruction of Japanese transport and supply infrastructure by Special Force. Ultimately, it was the official Japanese Defense Archives that noted that Wingate's Chindits 'greatly affected 33rd Army operations and eventually led to the total abandonment of North Burma'.

As a result of the Allied victory in Northern Burma, not only was the Japanese retreat from Imphal eastwards miserable due to a lack of supplies and transport, but it greatly contributed to the ability for Field Marshal Slim to launch his offensive into Central Burma after securing his victories at Imphal and Kohima. By early 1945, on the Arakan Peninsula in Burma's south-west, the British and Indians were now retaking land from the Japanese with great leaps towards Rangoon. In Central Burma, Slim's forces had crossed the Shwebo plain and were now arrayed near the Irrawaddy at several spots ready to entrap General Kimura's forces and secure victory at Meiktila and recapture Mandalay.

Although the Northern Burma campaign of 1943–44 has been mislabelled as a military backwater by some in contrast to other massive battlefields during the global conflict, it needs to be emphasized that Allied division and corps-sized forces engaged in deadly, protracted combat over several months at the extreme end of the logistical supply chain in some of the harshest terrain and climate imaginable.

As aptly summarized by Churchill in his memoirs: 'I disliked intensely the prospect of a large-scale campaign in Northern Burma. One could not choose a worse place for fighting the Japanese … We of course wanted to recapture Burma, but we did not want to have to do it by land advances from slender communications and across the most forbidding fighting country imaginable.'

An American Bofors anti-aircraft gun crew on alert along section of the Burma Road. Despite Myitkyina in Allied hands, Japanese planes attacked the road and Allied troop movements whenever possible. (*Nat. Arch. RG-208-AA-11P-2*)

(*Above*) With monsoon rains, mudslides down the Burmese hillsides were not uncommon and could often delay a column of trucks for lengthy intervals. (*USAMHI*)

(*Opposite above*) An American truck convoy along a stretch of the Ledo Road demonstrates how it was carved out of the vegetation of a Burmese hillside. (*Nat. Arch. 208-AA-11JJ-2PME*)

(*Opposite below*) A convoy of trucks crosses over a steel girder wooden plank bridge that crosses one of the numerous tortuous waterways in the Hukawng Valley. (*USAMHI*)

(*Above*) Troops of the American 96th Signal Battalion lay telephone cable along the Ledo Road at Mile Marker 9 in February 1944. (*Nat. Arch. 111-SC-263227*)

(*Opposite above*) A testimony to the engineering marvel of the Ledo Road builders under Brigadier Lewis Pick was the 960 foot span of the Tarung River Bridge in the Hukawng Valley. (*USAMHI*)

(*Opposite below*) When the juncture of the Ledo Road and Old Burma Road was completed, Chiang Kai-shek renamed the Ledo Road the Stilwell Road. (*USAMHI*)

STILWELL ROAD

LEDO • ASSAM

0•00

SHINGBWIYANG → 103		LUNGLING → 560		
WARAZUP → 189		PAOSHAN → 652		
MYITKYINA → 268		YUNGPING → 755		
BHAMO → 372		YUNNANYI → 876		
WANTING → 507		TSUYUNG → 958		

KUNMING → 1079

British generals salute their Burma victory with the capture of Mandalay. Field Marshal Slim is to the far right waving his hat to the cheering British and Indian troops. (USAMHI)

An American soldier in Mong Yu stands at the junction of the Ledo Road with the Old Burma Road, which proceeded to Wanting in China. (USAMHI)

One of the numerous pontoon bridges erected to cross the many waterways along the path of the Ledo Road as it traversed the Hukawng and Mogaung Valleys. (*USAMHI*)

Steel pipeline sections delivered to a rudimentary airstrip by a C-47 to assemble the fuel line bringing gasoline to keep Chiang's troops and Chennault's planes battling the Japanese. (*USAMHI*)

The civil engineer architect of the Ledo Road, Brigadier General Lewis Pick (*far left*) stands alongside SEAC leader Admiral Mountbatten (*second from left*) and other British officers at Ledo 7 April 1944. (*Nat. Arch. 111-SC-262504*)

A 2½-ton truck backs in supplies to a waiting C-47 transport to make the Hump Route to Yunnan Province in south-western China. (*USAMHI*)

The first truck convoy to traverse Pick's Pike enters Wanting, China in 1945. The distances to both Ledo and Kunming appear on the sign in the right foreground. *(USAMHI)*

American engineers race to complete a pontoon bridge across a wide Burmese waterway to enable Chinese troops and vehicles to move south towards their destination of Kamaing. *(USAMHI)*

(*Above*) Indian soldiers loading fuel barrels onto an ATC transport for the Hump Route flight from Assam to a Yunnan Province air terminal. (*USAMHI*)

(*Opposite page*) An Indian elephant and its handler load individual fuel barrels across the animal's tusks and trunk to an awaiting transport for air supply to China. (*USAMHI*)